KLAMATH
river angling guide

KLAMATH

river angling guide

George Burdick

Frank Amato Publications
P.O. Box 82112 • Portland, Oregon 97282
(503) 653-8108

Dedication

For my sister Lynn, whom
I've not seen since she was 10.

Book Design: Joyce Herbst • Typesetting: John Francis Michael
Cover Photos: Frank Amato, Joyce Sherman • Maps by Esther Poleo
ISBN 0-936608-88-9

Acknowledgements

Special thanks to my ex-wife Beth who typed my first article on a picnic table, beneath a redwood tree on the Klamath River. Thanks to Frank Amato for publishing that article and many more in *Salmon Trout Steelheader* and for giving me the opportunity to write my first book. Special mention to my friend Joe B. Clyburn whose photos of wildlife grace these pages and to Dan Brattan for letting me use his computer.

Thanks also to Ray Benner, Ron and Mike Benedict, Bill Claypole, Harold DelPonte, Don Duvol, Al Foss, Frank Gist, Elsie Gussin, Ron Gensaw, Ernie Hatton, Bud Johnson, Ed Hughes, Tim and Albert Kutzkey, Beverly Marsaw, Mable, Chub and Judy Morris, Bob Miles, Eleanor and John McMillan, Jim Roads, Phil Smith, Mark and Georgia Sanderson, Brad Throgmorton, Mable Westgard, Marvin Woods, Dorthy Williams, The Historical Societies of Del Norte and Siskiyou counties and the California Department of Fish and Game for sharing their statistics.

Lastly to Charlie Wick who faithfully typed the text of this manuscript.

Contents

Introduction

Research

Starting a project the magnitude of my first book brought many emotions covering the entire spectrum of ups and downs. In the beginning, a great deal of research is necessary and every avenue of acquiring facts must be explored. Items that cannot be substantiated need to be disregarded. Eventually the collection of collaborated facts form into ideas which I attempt to convey to you the reader, clearly and concisely. Setting these facts down in a logical format, arranging, rearranging, changing, moving whole chapters and trashing ideas, is the easy part.

Interviewing previously unknown people, being rejected, denied information, asked to pay for interviews, told deliberate falsehoods by glory seekers, no-show appointments and the loss of documents and pictures are the mine fields of research.

Choices

Authors have little choice in writing nonfiction; history is one of the truly unique adventures in writing. There should be a great deal of importance put on the correctness and credibility of events. Often there are two or more different stories of the same event. At times both have documentation in the form of letters, journals, newspapers or books. A choice must be made by the writer as to which way to present the facts. There are three basic choices: report it as you believe it to be; present both sides and write your way around it; or to simply let that one go by and not write about it at all.

Development

Eventually the format develops and the book takes shape. Chapters are finished first in rough, then final draft, still to be modified and changed when typed. Finally photos are collected, fit into the text, and the product reaches its final stage of development. If others write as I do, the introduction is written last. Still there are further problems when certain statements cannot be proved.

The History Of Requa

To give you a good example of how this process works there is no better story than the history of the naming of the town Requa.

The Facts

1. Long before any white man set eyes upon the Klamath River and long before Columbus discovered America the Yurok Indians had a village located at the mouth of the Klamath River. This village was named Rekwoi.

2. *Rekwoi* is the Yurok word that means the place where the fresh water meets the ocean.

3. The local Indians all say that the town name Requa was derived from the Yurok word *rekwoi* and reason, "who was here first?"

4. In 1887 a schooner from San Francisco named the *Requa* entered the Klamath River.

5. *The Family of Requa.* (Local people pronounce the present name of the town Re'qua.) There is a book in the Library of Congress of the same name and on page 32 it states: "John B. Requa moved to the mouth of the Klamath and founded a town for which he is named."

6. The same book mentions his brother who founded Piedmont, California but there is no mention of the schooner.

7. Local historians and members of the Del Norte Historical Society say that the town of Requa is named for the Requa family and not for the Indian village of Rekwoi.

8. Mrs. Jean Warnes of Eureka, California says that John B. Requa is her great uncle from Tarrytown, New York and that he founded the town of Requa and was a salmon trader.

9. From my research, John B. Requa came to the mouth of the Klamath, was a mining engineer and moved to Yreka where he became the county clerk of Siskiyou County.

It is only logical that the schooner *Requa* that came to the Klamath in 1887 was not named for the Indian village. And the spelling of the family name being the same as the town seems to be more than a coincidence.

There is a lot of conflict and only two plausible ways the town could have been named. Yet there can be no sure conclusions drawn and there will always be doubt.

Indian history is rarely written and depends on the handing down of stories. There always remains the basic human characteristic of changing stories each time they are told and retold. Rekwoi was an Indian village.

There is no way to form a complete conclusion! This story must either be disregarded or written in some sort of method such as the one I've used here in the introduction.

I have tried to give a fair and accurate view of what's happened on the Klamath River and to write about all those who deserve credit.

Incorporated in this text are complete life histories of the Klamath River's anadromous fish and the methods used to catch them. Also included are statistics to help the reader grasp the historical and current fluctuations of fish populations, the history of its fisheries, as well as the people involved. This is the beginning, the present and the future. The Klamath is a special place and it has given me more than any other geographic location, including the opportunity to write a book. I only hope these pages teach everyone something that they didn't know before about the Klamath River, its fish and its people. I would like to think I have given a little bit back... Thank you!

George Burdick

1 DISCOVERY AND DEVELOPMENT

Long before the first white fur trappers and explorers laid eyes on the Klamath River, the native people placed great importance on the salmon, steelhead, sturgeon, candle fish (smelt) and even the lamprey eels that ascend the waters of the Klamath River. (Skeletal remains of salmon have been found in archeological digs that were estimated to be 25,000 years old.)

There were four principal tribes that inhabited the Klamath River and its tributaries. The Yuroks ranged from the mouth of the river upstream about 45 miles to a boundary formed by Bluff Creek. The Hoopa ranged from the confluence of the Klamath and Trinity (Weitchpec), up the Trinity through a lovely valley that bordered the river. The Karoks inhabited the next 100 miles of the Klamath upstream from Bluff Creek, as well as much of the Salmon and Scott river drainages. The Shasta had their camps above this, near the present towns of Yreka and Hornbrook. Many areas had an intermingling of tribes, such as Fort Jones on the Scott River.

There were tribal conflicts, as well as family squabbles between rival families of the same tribe, usually caused by disputes over fish or fishing rights. The rugged terrain of the Klamath, however, kept contact to a minimum and the tribes lived in relative isolation for thousands of years.

One of the early fishing methods employed by the Indians was trapping salmon in weirs, built from woven branches and stone barriers. The tribe would herd a school of migrating salmon into the weir to be dispatched by spear or club.

Indian Ned salmon fishing on Klamath River. U.S. Census figures show Ned lived to be 116 years of age. Siskiyou Historical Society photo

Other methods such as nets, woven from wild iris, were used to catch the salmon. At Ishi Pishi Falls, the Karok tribe used baskets and iris-fiber nets attached to long handles of vine maple to "dip" the fish from the froth and white water as they struggled up and over this natural barrier.

Note: Ishi Pishi Falls is a heavy rapid strewn with numerous jagged rocks. It does not resemble a "water fall" by any imagination, it is more a huge rock pile that the river flows over.

Still further upstream, the salmon could be chased down in the confinement of small tributaries, speared, shot with an arrow or simply wrestled ashore. Anywhere along the river, migrating salmon might run into the work of industrious fishermen who built weirs to deceive and trap natures gift.

Discovery

Jedidiah Strong Smith was the first white man to reach the Klamath River by an overland route and arrived May 3, 1828 at the confluence of the Klamath and Trinity rivers. (During this period, the Trinity was labeled as Smith's River on many maps.) After a difficult and arduous trek through fog shrouded mountains, amid heavy spring rains in which some days only a mile in distance was achieved, Smith finally arrived at the lower river where he encountered many Indian camps.

Smith tried to persuade the Indians to take his party across the river with gestures and peaceful overtures. The Indians finally did take Smith across the river, but the real problem that day, according to Indian lore, was the filthy state of Smith's party. They stank, were streaked with dirt and had bugs crawling in the hair on their faces. After crossing the Klamath River, Smith's party headed north where they were attacked by Indians near the Umpqua River in Oregon. Smith and two others managed to escape, but Smith was eventually killed by Indians in the Southwest.

Reservation Land

With the arrival of explorers, fur trappers, gold seekers, pioneers and settlers, change came quickly to the native people. Their long isolation and way of life began to change even more with the establishment of the Klamath Indian Reservation on November 16, 1855 and the building of Fort Ter Wah in 1857. Indian agents were sent to aid the tribe in the instruction of members in "various duties and pursuits which their relocation might necessitate." One H.B. Dickenson was hired by Indian agent S. G. Whipple to proceed in this endeavor. Dickenson took farm tools, seeds and twine for "fish nets." (This may well have been the first time Indians used anything other than the fiber of wild iris for their nets.) At this time, there were reported to be some 1,500 Indians living on the reservation.

The native religion, which worshipped all things as living entities including rocks, had a legend about a large, uniquely shaped rock standing at the mouth of the Klamath River, "Oregos," the guardian of the river's salmon and whose very spirit guided the fish on the journey to the sea and back to the river of their birth. The people showed their reverence and cooked the flesh of the salmon on redwood stakes over a slow fire of alder chips. The salmon were the food and the river was the life blood of the people.

Mark Sanderson with a 13-1/2 pound steelhead caught at McCovey Pool, Klamath River, 1988. Frank Duarte photo

Many tribes would gather together at times of religious ceremonies. Indians from the Smith River, Crescent City and Redwood Creek would journey to the Klamath for the "White Deer Skin Dance" or the "Brush Dance."

A letter dated February 8, 1874, from the Klamath pioneers to the U.S. Congress, asked the question: "If land formerly occupied as an Indian reservation at the mouth of the Klamath River has been abandoned is the land open to settlement as any other unsurveyed government land?" Congressmen tried to have the reservation land released to settlement; the citizens of Del Norte County also petitioned for its release. Meanwhile settlers took advantage of this confusing situation and built homes and made other improvements on reservation land.

The White Deer Skin Dance. Del Norte Historical Society photo

Whose Reservation?

Interaction between the whites and Indians has run a long course of racial problems, because civilization and ancient ways have bumped heads for over 150 years. Just as most of the conflicts between the tribes involved disputes over fish and fishing rights, the problems between whites and Indians usually involved the salmon and the wealth they brought. There was also another major controversy that has lived on and is still in court under litigation today: that of whose reservation it is? It is a question that began in the 1870s and has remained undecided for over 100 years.

Many of the Klamath (Yurok) Indians were transferred to the Smith River Reservation or permanently relocated on the Hoopa Reservation on the Trinity River from 1875 through 1876.

On November 21, 1877 came an order from the Department of the Interior that read, "By order **all white men** living on the Klamath Indian Reservation have been ordered to move off, forthwith!"

On December 19, 1877 extension time was given to the 20 or so settlers who had offered it to be a "hardship" to move off of the Indian land.

In 1884, a bill was introduced by Senator Barclay Henry for the restoration of the reservation to public lands. The bill failed.

On April 23, 1887 the *Del Norte Record* reports: "The woods are full of *LAND GRABBERS*! Three or four claimants to every 160 acre parcel of land!"

In 1894 the Klamath Indian Reservation was legally and officially, "opened and prepared to receive application for homesteads."

By 1978, all reservation and native fishing rights had been restored to the members of the Yurok and Hoopa tribes. Along with this reacquisition of reservation land came the never ending question of: "Whose reservation?" The debate still continues in 1989: how to divide the reservation between the Hoopa and Yurok tribes.

Gill Net Fishing

The netters began arriving at sunset, quickly broke up into small groups and began to unload small wooden boats. They would be fishing far into the night for Chinook salmon that were entering their native river. The nets were set and I had to admire the skill with which they were rowed into place. Each Indian kept an eye on his net; quick excited cries greeted each salmon strung in the gill nets. The monofilament line sounded in sharp twangs as the salmon were wrestled into the boats.

A gill net looks a lot like a volleyball net. The bottom net line (lead) is weighted to hug the bottom. The top line is a float line (cork) and the net stretches from top to bottom across all but the deepest holes in the river. Length can be up to 100 feet, but most nets are shorter, using too long a net for the eddy being fished is akin to using too heavy tackle to suit the conditions. The net itself is usually monofilament from 18 to 35-pound test, in four to eight ply (it can be up to 12 strands). Four ply, 35-pound test has 140 pounds of break strength. The mesh size, or area of each square in the net can vary according to what size or kind of fish is being fished. Most meshes are 7 1/4 inches for Chinook, 5 1/2 inches for steelhead and 9 1/2 inches when targeting sturgeon.

Commercial salmon fishing has returned to the Klamath River and in 1987 and '88 Indians were allowed to gill-net salmon for sale. Here Alton and Chad Haberman, father and son, show the 44 salmon "netted" in a nights work. Salmon sold for $2.10 per pound. Dorothy Haberman photo

Future Thoughts

In 1987, the first in-river commercial fishery since 1928 allowed Indian gill netters to harvest 29,000 fall-run Chinook to be sold to one central buyer. (This allowed for a fair and accurate count.) An additional 28,000 fall Chinook were allowed to be netted for Indian subsistence. Legal sales of the salmon for top dollar provided individual netters with a source of income. A percentage of each netter's earnings was taken by the tribe for its own use. (Hopefully this money will be used to improve fisheries.)

Still there are continued questions voiced by many people as to the legitimacy of Indian net rights. Instead of dealing with gill netting, pro or con, we should give thought to better management. Instead of harvesting the entire commercial quota from the first salmon that enter the river, the netting period should alternate closed periods to provide a better division of spawning salmon to Klamath and Trinity river tributaries. In 1987, 199,000 Chinook entered the Klamath River; 53,000 were harvested by gill nets while 44,000 adult Chinook continued on to the Klamath and its tributaries; leaving 85,500 adult Chinook to overflow the Trinity River. (Note: The remaining 16,500 adult Chinook were the total for the 1987 sport catch on the river.) It would seem a much better plan to regulate the gill net harvest for a better escapement division in the tributaries because the timing of the two runs differs and is documented by fisheries biologists.

Some small changes in the gill net regulations, such as allowing only resident Indians netting rights, regulation of mesh size to target on specific age class salmon and most importantly to make net attendance mandatory in the lower river below Blake's Riffle would be a step in the right direction. Net attendance in the lower river would go a long way in discouraging harbor seals and sea lions from gorging on the easy pickings found lodged in the mesh.

No one should be naive enough to think the removal or ban of Indian gill nets would be a fast fix to declining salmon populations. It should be pointed out that ocean commercial fisheries have harvested 84 percent (average) of yearly Klamath River salmon runs. Besides the numbers of harvested fish, the shaker (immature salmon) mortality should be taken into account. It can be as much as 20 percent of the average yearly in-river run, or as in 1982, an estimated 60,000 fish. The past two years have provided proof that the ocean troll is where we are killing tremendous numbers of salmon. Cutbacks in the KMZ (Klamath Management Zone) per 1986/87 have directly increased the number of fall Chinook entering the Klamath River.

Whatever the future holds, some changes are in order. The ocean troll has to face hard times and smaller harvests. An unregulated, unlimited gill net fishery cannot be maintained on the river. Guides need to practice conservation. We

Fishing the mouth of the Klamath. Del Norte Historical Society photo

must all get past the racism that keeps us pushing against each other so we can work together to cross some of the bridges over this troubled water.

Commercial Fisheries At The Mouth Of The Klamath

Early pioneers enjoyed a grand misconception when the first ships found the mouth of the Klamath River to be navigable. Large numbers of gold seekers, pioneers and settlers were brought by steamer from San Francisco to fast growing Klamath. This notion of a year-round harbor and rapid growth was proclaimed in papers throughout the state. The *Pacific Daily News* of San Francisco carried idyllic images of the area: "The climate is beautiful...no high winds, heavy dew, or chilly nights to which San Francisco is subject. Vessels are now running from San Francisco to the Klamath River and a line of steamers will soon be put on the route. The Klamath River affords a safe and excellent harbor at all times capable of ingress and egress to the heaviest shipping."

The first realizations that the changing mouth of the Klamath would make entrance difficult came with the first high water. As the water receded, the entire mouth was blocked to passage by "shifting sands."

From the *Del Norte Record*, January 1851: "Vessels are waiting for spring before attempting to cross the bar."

Spring found the river bar still impossible to be navigated and the town of Klamath City was abandoned before it was one year old. Twenty-nine people lost their lives that year due to drowning or trouble with the Indians.

From the journal of Thomas Gihon, miner and pioneer, June 18, 1850: "The river seemed alive with salmon and seals, yet here in this hidden place was going on the interminable war, the struggle for existence. A seal would dive and presently appear with a salmon in its mouth, which he would thrash upon the water breaking it to pieces. Then a cloud of gulls would swoop down upon him and seize the pieces so that though surrounded with plenty, he had to fight for the little he got, like common humanity."

With this abundance of salmon it was only natural for white immigrants to capitalize and commercialize that which "the Lord had provided." European ideas came with the immigrants to this new land. As the wagons and ships brought progress ever westward, the pioneers stared wide-eyed saying to themselves, "it's all mine." However, Indians had lived here for thousands of years.

Part of the catch at the Klamath Packing and Trading Company, the largest cannery on the Klamath River. Del Norte Historical Society photo

The first commercial cannery was established on the Klamath River in August of 1877 by Martin Jones and George Richardson. It was a very small cannery/saltery, and during its entire length of operation it was necessary to maintain a constant vigil against the Indians who resented this looting of fish from the river they had always lived upon. It was also operated without permission on reservation land and received pressure to close.

During the same year John Bomhoff secured permission from Indian Agent S. G. Whipple to build a cannery near the mouth of the Klamath.

Commercial harvest in 1913 at the mouth of the Klamath River. Del Norte Historical Society photo

Still later in 1877, a scow from Gold Beach, Oregon owned by R.D. Hume, anchored in the mouth of the Klamath with a house built on board and equipment and complete machinery to carry on the merchandising, salting and canning of fish. This entire outfit was seized by the U.S. Marshall in 1888 and removed from the river. It was later returned to the owner and sailed back to Gold Beach.

Bomhoff and Hume, after much competition, became partners and began a new cannery under the name of "The Klamath Packing and Trading Co." In 1889, the company was reported to have shipped 1,200 barrels of salmon to San Francisco markets in its first year of operation. (Fish and Game data of the commercial canneries on the Klamath River showed that this single company, The Klamath Packing and Trading Co., harvested an average of 90 percent of the river's salmon by weight.)

From the *Del Norte Record*, October 5, 1889: "The fishermen of Klamath have formed a union."

June 27, 1891: "The can labeling machine invented by Henry Albert of the Klamath River has proved to be a success. Vulcan Iron Works of San Francisco has just completed one of the machines and has received orders from the syndicate who handles the machines for nine more of the same style." July 10, 1897: "The shipping of fresh salmon from the Klamath River to San Francisco is likely to be discontinued as only 1-1/2 cents per pound is being paid for salmon in San Francisco markets."

All of the canneries were located near the mouth of the river in the growing community of Requa, which was separate and originally larger than Klamath and boasted the only post office between the two towns for many years. (Eventually Requa and Klamath merged as simply Klamath.) The largest of the canneries was owned by the Klamath Packing & Trading Co. with offices in San Francisco. There was also the Requa Fishery Co. and several other smaller packing and salting operations at the mouth of the Klamath.

Salmon fishing for the canneries was done, by Indian netters and a few Swedes, in the estuary. Each day the cannery whistle blew to begin the fishing and watchful eyes kept track of the salmon being boated by the derby hatted fishermen. When enough fish were caught to keep the cannery working all day the whistle blew again to end the day's fishing. Netters would often catch the day's quota in one or two hours.

The commercial fishery flourished on the lower Klamath River for about 50 years. In the 1920s, sport fishing interests campaigned for its closure and 1928 was the last year of commercial salmon fishing in the river.

A Department of Fish & Game bulletin covered the final 14 years not only in terms of fish caught but also a ratio of fish per boat by recording the average number of boats fishing each year. In 1915 there were 40 boats fishing and they caught 1,232,229 pounds for a 30,805 pounds per boat average. However in 1928, there were 126 boats fishing and the per boat average dropped to 2,451 pounds per boat. This steady decline documented the need to close the commercial fishing in the Klamath River.

Out of curiosity as to how many fish the numbers of pounds represented, I divided 1915's 1,232,229 pounds by 15 pounds (estimated average weight of a salmon) and it equalled 82,148 salmon.

The State Of Klamath

At one time part of northern California was occupied by a large shallow sea, surrounded by a rugged land mass known as Siskiyou Island. This sea supported marine life such as clams, ammonites, turritellas and sharks. Fossils of these organisms provide the major frame of reference in recognizing time from a geological perspective.

After the initial excitment caused by the discovery of "gold" at Sutter's Mill in 1848, the rest of the state of California was quickly staked,

Commercial Salmon Catch Statistics From 1915 to 1928.

YEAR	SALMON IN POUNDS	NUMBER OF BOATS
1915	1,232,229	40
1916	801,150	
1917	265,537	
1918	672,345	
1919	535,198	
1920	872,295	
1921	614,247	
1922	1,039,580	
1923	824,291	
1924	814,572	
1925	956,082	
1926	811,714	
1927	408,081	
1928	308,826	126

filed and claimed by prospectors looking for riches. Many times these miners were the first whites the Indians encountered. It was along the upper Klamath River and its tributaries (Shasta, Scott, Salmon and Trinity rivers) that much of the placer, or hydraulic mining took place. It was also the presence of gold that gave these early northern Californians the idea (and power) to attempt to divide the state in half, calling the northern half Klamath State.

The *Yreka Herald*, in December of 1853 suggested forming Klamath into a state. "The distance and lack of investment from population centers in Southern California along with the abundant water system of the Klamath Drainage, along with gold to insure growth surely gives cause for Klamath to become a state."

Nine years later efforts were still under way to divide the state, on June 9, 1864 the *Alta California* reported: "The Klamath is larger than the Sacramento and small steamers might ascend it for 20 or 30 miles."

This proved to be wrong. Not only was the Klamath second in size to the Sacramento, but also the shifting sands at the mouth caused shippers to abandon the idea of a safe harbor. The rapid depletion of the gold proved too much, and an end came to the idea of Klamath as a state.

The Gold Mines

Upriver, the gold fields and mines were in their heyday from 1850 through the early 1900s with many mines continuing to operate into the 1950s when legislation ended hydraulic mining in California.

There were basically four mining methods: placer or hydraulic, hard rock, panning and dredging. Of these methods, it was hydraulic mining that cost the future of fisheries for time untold. Huge sites were mined with giant nozzles that shot streams of water – washing away the topsoil in order to mine the sand and gravel tail-

A wing-dam mine on the Klamath River across from Long Gulch in the 1890s. Note the dip wheel in the background (farthest upstream) which is bringing water up to the trestled flume. The flume conveys the water to a sluice which discharges it over the top of the dam. The current wheel in the fore-ground powers a pump. The large piles of rock in the center of the picture were stacked with the aid of the derrick. Siskiyou Historical Society photo

A 9 inch nozzle washes away topsoil and this barren rock remains, forever barren. The Dump Giant Mine of Siskiyou County. Siskiyou Historical Society photo

ings underneath. Some nozzles were as large as 9 inches, like the ones used for the LaGrange Mine on the Trinity River.

The water needed for these efforts came from engineering marvels. It was carried via ditches, pipes, forced upstream into impoundments behind wing dams, up giant siphons, across bridges, along trestles – as long and as far as the water could be carried to a waiting nozzle. The Trinity Gold Placer Mining Syndicate constructed a 500-foot tunnel used to obtain the necessary water pressure to mine the tailings of their rich claim. Water to wash away the earth, leaving bare scars that never healed; sending silt downstream to the lower Klamath River. Mines like the Siskiyou Mining Co., Black Bear, Evening Star, Know Nothing, Hard Rock, Central Mountain Laurel, Gold Run and Live Yankee attacked the land with their hydraulic nozzles, leaving huge piles of rock along the upper portions of every stream in the Klamath River system.

The Consequences

Over many years the vast areas of land mined by the hydraulic method have played havoc with downstream fishing. When the mines were operating, anglers were forced to fish the clearing water near the edges of the river and many a story mentions the fact that when the mines were shut down every year in July, the fishing would also begin.

Today we are still paying the price of this massive streamside degradation caused by hydraulic mining. The loss of land mass above the gravel bars created endless gravel to be easily exposed to the yearly high water and washed downstream. It allowed a much more rapid exchange of gravel between the upper and lower river, to the point today of gravel depletion in upstream spawning beds and the filling in of the lower river with this same gravel. This gravel saturation in the lower river has caused a widening of the river, loss in the needed velocity for flushing action, and the deprivation of needed rearing habitat for downstream migrants in the estuary.

There are a few dredges still operating throughout the Klamath River system. The permits are issued and overseen by the Department of Fish and Game with an eye to the welfare of our fisheries and the quality of the river. We can all be certain that the practice of hydraulic gold mining will never be used again on the rivers of California.

A dredger on the Klamath in the 1800s. Siskiyou Historical Society photo

Lumbermen

Imagine the thoughts that went through the minds of the first white settlers as their gaze met *Sequoia sempervirens*, the redwood standing over 200-feet tall with trunks sometimes over 15 feet in diameter. No other tree in the world compares in size or majestic shape to the giant redwood tree of California. I'm sure every Easterner or former European immigrant was calculating the board feet; the number of houses in a single tree or simply the stack of wood no other tree could equal. (The belt of redwoods extended inland only 10 to 20 miles from the sea.)

Upriver there were also very large quantities of fir and pine that were beheld by early pioneers and pronounced as "surely inexhaustible." From the *Del Norte Record*, August 1880: "The banks of the Klamath are bordered with some of the best timber in the country. On the south side of the river is the best of redwood, interspersed with white cedar, 25 miles in extent. On the north it extends for about 8 miles and upriver are quantities of fir and pine to satisfy any market."

The first sawmill in Klamath was owned by the Klamath Commercial Company and promoted by R. D. Hume. (Also of Klamath Packing and Trading Company, a cannery.) Built in the Hunter Creek area near Requa in 1881, it shipped lumber to Crescent City for further reshipment to San Francisco. By 1894 there were three sawmills in Klamath and soon another in Requa operated by Ed Hughes.

The men who cut the trees, set the wedges, and stepped astride a spring board to fall one of these giants and cry "TIMBER" were cut from leather and stone. There was a bond, a feeling of exhilaration in the felling of these monstrous trees and a power in the act – ego in felling every tree. Men say it is hard work and indeed it is, but so often fallers admit receiving pleasure when they see the speed gather, hear the air roar and the crash that comes with each and every tree they cut down.

Tugboats

As the logging moved upriver, further and further from town, the best and most obvious means was to use the river as a conduit to carry the timber downstream to be loaded and taken to market. From the steep hills, small streams flowed down to the river. These were used to float the logs to the river or if too shallow, the logs would be dragged through the creek bed. Once in the river, logs were bound together to form a raft and were pulled downstream to the reloader by tugboats. From that point they were hauled by truck to the mill.

In order for the propeller powered tugboats to navigate the shallow riffles, two methods were used to open passage: that of simply prop washing the channel (running the motor at high RPMs above the shallows to break gravel loose and flush it downstream), or hauling a cat upriver by barge and constructing wing dams to raise the water level. The practice of prop washing channels was quickly discontinued due to downstream complaints of muddy water. The Klamath is well remembered as a deep river from the '30s till the '60s when the depletion of harvestable trees made tugboats a thing of the past. People still talk about those days when there were many more boats upriver than there are today. Jet boats were unnecessary and any propeller powered craft could head upstream throughout the year. Tugboat operator Ernie Baumgardner once counted over "two thousand lines (anchor) in the lower three miles of the river." Today there are usually under 200 boats upriver on any given day. The tugboat era lasted 30 odd years and records indicate from 1952 through 1964 more than 400 million board feet of timber was rafted down the Klamath River.

Tugboats like these hauled the rafts of logs down the Klamath River. Over 400 million board feet of timber passed down the Klamath River from 1950 to 1964. Marvin Wood photo

Log Jams, Slash Piles And Erosion

How did this logging affect the fisheries? The clear- cuts left the earth open and exposed, first to wind erosion and then water erosion. As soil was washed away in the heavy winter rains it left the land scarred and barren. Stream banks were destroyed by the intrusion of heavy equipment driven through the creeks without regard to the destruction of rearing and spawning habitat of salmon and steelhead. Shade trees that protected small streams from the sun were felled and left in order to gain access to fir and redwood. Many times these deciduous trees would form logjams blocking migration of anadromous species. Other streams were blocked by slides caused by erosion from poor logging practices. Slash-piles were often left to remain as debris washed downstream in the next high water.

Better Management Through Legislation

New regulations and sweeping legislation have changed many past practices of the timber industry. Today's foresters are, by and large, more conscious of consequences and better educated in fishery needs. There are set distances (200 feet) that form protective boundaries along streams and rivers for both logging and spraying of defoliant by lumber companies. (The spraying is done to retard growth of deciduous trees so that conifers can gain needed sunlight. It does not "kill" the trees but only denudes them, leaving huge "dead" appearing areas in the Klamath scenery.) Aggressive reforestation has also been implemented by far-seeing lumber companies as well as new methods for achieving faster growing "starter" trees for planting.

Lumber has been the backbone of the economy along the Klamath River. It outlasted the gold mining by many years as a source of jobs and revenue. Early estimates of an unlimited timber supply were far from correct and today's companies face economic instability and political pressure from unions and environmentalists. Present tax base structures are also a problem when they conflict with logical harvest practices. At times taxes levied on standing timber force harvest and many companies are going broke, cutting back or just throwing in the towel and closing their mills.

Bald Eagle high atop a sugar pine in the upper Klamath River area of Siskiyou County. Joe B. Clyburn photo

2 Flood Stage

Like a great terror devouring all in its path, the Klamath River is legendary for its "hell and high water"; ruining the dreams of many, and destroying the work of lifetimes.

Someone once said: "The Lord giveth and the river taketh away."

Since records have been kept, the Klamath River has known many a major flood and rises to flood stage are common along its entire length. In every flood the loss of property and personal possessions as well as human life has been the price paid for living too close to its banks. Many are the hardships and losses for those who chose to live inside the flood plain. The years between floods often built false senses of security among residents. Time let many believe that "it surely couldn't happen again." Stores, homes, roads and bridges were rebuilt only to be washed away again in the fury and rage the Klamath River knows at flood stage.

The first recorded flood on the Klamath occurred in the winter of 1861-1862 when the weather turned bad and northern California was pelted by ceaseless rain. The few area roads were washed away and travel became nearly impossible. Reports of drownings at many of the stream crossings shut down mail delivery and the Klamath country was cut off from the outside world.

The *San Francisco Bulletin* ran a letter received from a Crescent City correspondent dated December 18, 1861:

"I wrote you about two weeks ago by mail, giving you some account of the ravages of the storm in the vicinity. Since then, we have had a second rise and received news from places we had not then heard from. The news from the Klamath, so far as received, fully justifies our worst apprehensions, as expressed in my last letter. On the first rise, all enlisted quarters at Fort Ter-Waw, 20 in number were carried away and on the second rise, three used as officers quarters were carried away. As were all the improvements on the Indian reservation. All the stores of every description at the fort were lost, except the flour and the beef cattle.

"Communications are so cut off that we have not heard from any of the headwaters of the Klamath. We only judge what the devastation must have been by what we find strewing the beach here. For eight miles, which is conveniently accessible, the beach is covered to an average width of 200 yards and to a depth of three to ten feet with every description of material that can be found in the countryside, except gold. One large officers tent was picked up a few days ago. Winter squash in good order are occasionally found. Goods of all sorts, but badly damaged are often seen. The best of timber lies on the beach in quantities to supply the markets of California for years. White cedar, sugar pine, redwood and red and yellow fir are as plentiful as blackberries in summer."

This description gave a good idea as to the disaster on the Klamath. The new town of Klamath City was also severely damaged as well as many Indian "rancherias" along the river.

The next flood occurred on the river in 1881

and was said to be much larger than the flood of 1861-1862. *The Del Norte Record* on January 22, 1881 reported:

"M.G. Tucker of the Klamath, reports on the Klamath River, from which we learn that the river rose to an unprecedented height, sweeping everything from within its reach. Huge trees that had uprooted from the banks came crashing down the river, some of which were deposited on the farms while others found their way to the ocean. Houses were swept away and considerable stock drowned. Some places where the grain was growing green a few days ago, are now covered with debris. Such a flood, says Tucker, was never known before; the water was higher than the winter of 1861-1862."

There is thought to be a cycle of floods that repeat on a regular basis. Scientific theory has drawn flood plains based on 10-year and 100-year floods. This pattern, though not exact, has been seen on the northern coastal streams of California. The Klamath has had several floods that came nine years apart as well as an 1861 and 1964 flood, 103 years apart. In keeping with that time cycle, nine years after the flood of 1881, another flood struck the Klamath and this flood, too, was bigger than the last.

The *Del Norte Record,* December 1890 reports: "Hunters Creek country was submerged during the recent storm by the backwater of the Klamath River. In low places the water was 10 feet deep. At Martin's Ferry the river rose 100 feet, the highest ever known."

As a child, I remember old timers talking about the winter of 1890 and no matter how bad the weather seemed to me they'd always say, "This is nothing compared to the winter of 1890." Indeed, there were many storms and seasons of heavy rains. There were floods of not so devastating a proportion and throughout the years, the Klamath has maintained its reputation as a moody river capable of turning its wrath loose upon those who live near its shores.

Ferries And Bridges

For many years, the unstable nature of the Klamath hampered travel; restricting it to times of normal water levels when crossings were safe – first for horse or boat, and then ferry. Ferries operated on the Klamath River for 50 years in periods of stable flow. Such was the formidable barrier imposed by the waters of the Klamath River.

The first ferry permit was granted to M.G. Tucker on September 2, 1876 by the Del Norte County Board of Supervisors for permission to "erect a ferry and collect a toll" on the Klamath River. This ferry was located about one-half mile above the mouth and proved to be a great improvement on travel both north and south along the coast. The ferry operated through Indian trouble, shifting mouths, high waters and the wear and tear of use. Just 10 years later the ferry had fallen into a state of disrepair and was reported being run by an Indian ferryman famous for his non-appearance.

By this time there were several ferries operating along the Klamath upriver from the mouth. One of these, Martin's Ferry, gave access to the Trinity gold fields and operated successfully for many years.

In 1895 another ferry was constructed at the mouth of the Klamath River by stretching a 1700 foot cable across the river. This was some 300 feet longer than the Eel River Ferry cable. (Note: Due to the ferries on the Eel andKlamath rivers a popular expression among the people, There's no law north of the Eel and no God north of the Klamath was often said, due to the isolation and remoteness of the region.) This ferry was operated by William Baily and Charles Fortain for about 20 years before it was worn out, neglected and in a very poor state of repair.

In June 1919, the *Del Norte Triplicate* reported: "A new contract has been given to Dave Ball and Stacey Fisher." Ball was to build the ferry and Mr. Fisher was to be the operator. This ferry was replaced seven years later by the Douglas Memorial Bridge.

The following excerpt is from the Klamath River Bridge dedication speech on May 17, 1926:

"The bridging of the Klamath River has long been an ambition of the engineers of the California Highway Commission. Surveys, studies and soundings have been made during the past 10 years, preliminary to deciding upon the type of bridge and the proper location. The Douglas Bridge now spans the Klamath about three miles from its mouth at a point where the river is nearly a quarter of a mile wide. Heretofore, the river has been crossed by a small ferry which could not be operated at times of extreme high or low water. Steel was the structural material first considered for construction of the bridge, but when the memorial features were introduced, it was decided the structure should be of concrete. The bridge consists of five main arch spans, each 210 feet in length with short approach spans at each end. In some respects, the structure is unique and the only one of its kind in the world. Much objection was presented by engineers to prove the impossibility of bridging the wild flood waters of the Klamath River with concrete arches; the current was too swift, the floods were too great, the drift too heavy (frequently full sized redwood trees, some as great as 15 feet in diameter are forced down the river with their roots dragging). The final decision was made for a bold design incorporating mounting the concrete arches on deep piles surrounded and protected by cofferdams driven to the point of refusal in the sand and gravel at the bottom of the river. Carefully checked measurements were constantly under way during construction and the centers were struck in the false work without any apparent settlement of the arches. The bridge will stand for all time as a suitable and beautiful memorial to Dr. Douglas."

Of course it is true that forever only lasts until the next time the river exceeds flood stage on the Klamath River. The Douglas Memorial Bridge was only to last 38 years before it was washed away in the 1964 flood. The bridge did withstand many small floods including the 1955 flood which washed away the north approach to the bridge. Its final demise was one foreseen by engineers; huge logs that washed against the bridge eventually carried the center span downstream.

Dr. Douglas was a long time river resident who for years campaigned for the bridging of the Klamath.

Aerial photo showing the mouth of the Klamath. Jim Hopelain photo

In Klamath It's A "Wet Christmas"

Though many floods have affected the Klamath River basin and its inhabitants, there were two floods that still stand out in people's minds. These two came crashing down the creeks and canyons of the tributaries, blowing out roads, carrying away bridges and leaving entire towns in muddy ruin. They affected the lives of many of the people living on the Klamath today: destroying homes, carrying away personal possessions, and dashing dreams forever. These two floods occurred almost nine years apart to the day: Christmas Eve 1955 and the night before Christmas Eve in 1964. The floods of 1955 and 1964 were the two most costly floods to ravage the Klamath River.

1955 Flood

The 1955 flood made Christmas a disaster that won't soon be forgotten. High water took its toll all along the river but most of the damage, as is usually the case, was reported in the lower river with the town of Klamath hardest hit.

Downtown Klamath would never be the same. Main Street was ripped and torn apart leaving pavement strewn about to attest to the force of the flood waters! The new Chevron station was a shambles, Brizzard's Department Store and the U.S. Post Office located in the same building were destroyed with fully one half of the store washed away. The famous Redwood Room was torn apart and smashed into the front of the 777 Club. The new Robinet Mill was lost along with many other area mills. The new elementary school in Klamath was under 10 feet of water and the north approach to the Douglas Memorial Bridge (Highway 101) was washed out leaving the highway closed. Many residents were left out in the cold on the Eve of Christmas.

Houses in Klamath Glen were but shells – some with uprooted foundations broken and crumbling. The McBeth subdivision had most of its homes in place though they were filled with silt and mud. The river bar and land from the airstrip down, was totally denuded with only two of the 40 houses that were once there still in place.

Upriver many homes and lodges were washed away and left only as memories in the minds of those who knew them. In Hoopa the Indian reservation was hard hit by devastation never known before in that beautiful valley on the Trinity. The Humboldt Fir Lumber Co. mill was hard struck; airplanes from the landing strip were swept away and left lodged, broken and torn in the trees along the river bank. Many ranches lost stock. The Indians were homeless and without food and supply routes were wiped out. The only way to ease the plight of the people in Hoopa was the air drop performed by the Red Cross.

The 1955 Christmas Eve flood destroyed Blue Creek Lodge. In this photo the main lodge had slipped down the bank only to be carried away in the second rise on January 15. Blue Creek Lodge photo

One Family's Loss

Also lost in the 1955 flood was the famous Blue Creek Fishing Lodge, run by Jack and Mable Morris.

A newsletter by Jack Morris called *The Blue Creek Herald* on January 20, 1956 stated:

"Starting with a wind of near hurricane velocity, followed by torrential rains, the river started to rise slowly on Wednesday before Christmas... The rise was slow and as usual, I was watching and measuring. Seven inches in five hours but after dinner a check on the measuring stick showed a rise of 18 inches. From that point on everyone tried to salvage what they could.

"Our lodge also received a complete going over. (The Morris family home in Klamath Glen had also been badly damaged.) The hill unit alone being there along with the laundry building and one other small single room cabin. The dining room and house survived to the extent of just sliding down the hill to the bar. However, during the big rise we had on January 15, we saw the house go by under the 101 (Douglas Memorial) Bridge and I feel that the dining room must have floated out in the night."

The Morris family lost the lodge they had operated nearly 20 years, consisting of 38 cabins, a laundry house and dining room, as well as having their house in the Klamath Glen gutted and filled with silt. They also lost all of their photos, address books and the acquired possessions dear to them. In spite of this, Jack Morris closed the final edition of his newsletter, *The Blue Creek Herald* with these words:

"One thing the flood can never reach are the memories we have of watching Blue Creek Lodge grow. It was a hell of a lot of work, a great deal more fun and a host of really swell friends. Whatever Mable and I do we plan on staying in this area, so if you get up this way, look us up... After all, friends are really such great gadgets."

The 1964 Flood

The rebuilding of the Klamath River valley seemed hardly finished – foundations of new businesses and homes barely settled – when the "flood to end all floods" struck the Klamath River almost nine years to the day after the disaster of 1955. In 1964, the river experienced its most devastating flood. A combination of a heavy snow pack followed by warm tropical storms brought unheard of amounts of water rushing

The Klamath in the 1955 flood. Photo courtesy of John McMillan

down every gully and stream to produce a raging torrent of proportions never known before on the Klamath River.

Water poured over the spillway at Iron Gate Dam causing the upper river to rage in a white froth of newly forming rapids. Islands disappeared as banks overflowed, filling houses and lodges along the river. And the famous Kutzkey Lodge was inundated by the rapidly rising Klamath River.

Near Hornbrook, a huge three level dredge broke loose taking bridges out at Klamathon and Highway 99. The sway bridge in between had miraculously survived as it swayed, twisted, teetered and bent to allow the huge dredge by.

Flood-ravaged Siskiyou County reeled in the wake of the Klamath River's awesome power, the county west of highway 99 was virtually without roads. People in Yreka reported muddy water in their faucets and the *Yreka Herald* advised residents to boil their water.

The Shasta River screamed into the Klamath, sending huge volumes of debris filled, muddy water downstream. Trees floated everywhere as the wall of water snapped scrub oak and cottonwood like match sticks. Many of the area's bridges were lost due to the accumulation of logs and debris upstream creating tremendous pressure. A huge jam of logs backed up behind the Horse Creek Bridge before it cracked under the pressure caused by the tons of lumber.

On the Scott River, melting snow packs brought fir and pine hurtling down, washing out the approach to the Scott Valley Bridge and destroying the Quartz Valley Bridge and flooding the entire Scott Valley.

Still further down the Klamath, Happy Camp was nearly underwater and much of the town evacuated. At Orleans, the hotel had chest-deep water in the lobby and highway 96 was washed out making travel in or out impossible. Near Bluff Creek a wall of water, some say 100 feet high, washed away highway 96 and made a new mouth for the creek.

Quartz Valley Bridge, Scott River Aerial view, 1964 after flood. Note the snow pack that remained even after warm rains flooded the river. Siskiyou Historical Society photo

The Bluff Creek Story

One of the living legends of the Klamath River, Al Foss, told me this story about Bluff Creek and its total destruction in the 1964 flood:

"Way back up Bluff Creek Country, above Fish Lake in the heavy timber, there had been quite a bit of cat logging going on. Cat logging was notorious for its rip and tear methods and they'd (the loggers) left huge piles of slash and smaller trees behind. A large depression was formed into a huge lake with the slash acting as a dam holding back acres of water. This finally broke away filling Fish Lake and washing it into Bluff Creek. A torrent of water 100 feet high roared down this beautiful creek destroying everything in its path. When it got to Highway 96, it just up and ate a hole through the hillside, devouring the highway and making a new mouth for Bluff Creek upstream from its former mouth.

"Now, Bluff Creek steelhead were something special and the creek itself had some 15 miles of the best spawning habitat anywhere on the Klamath. All of this was destroyed in the devastation the 1964 flood reeked on Bluff Creek. The new mouth also flowed over huge boulders making an almost impassible barrier for steelhead. It's a real shame because the Bluff Creek strain held some of the largest genetic stock the Klamath River ever knew, with many of the steelhead in the 12 to 15 pound range. All this was lost. The 1964 flood was the single most devastating incident to affect the steelhead fishing on the Klamath River."

NOTE: Presently there is a rebuilding effort for this great strain of steelhead being spearheaded by Al Foss and is covered in detail in Chapter 6.

Below Somes Bar to Weitchpec where the Trinity River entered the Klamath the most devastating effects of the flood were felt. Waters reached incredible heights and homes that had stood along the banks through other floods of the Klamath for 100 years or more were quickly gone forever.

Lower River And Klamath Destroyed!

In the cycle of floods there is also said to be a thousand year flood. Perhaps the tremendous flood of 1964 was in fact the thousand year flood and will not be repeated for many centuries. Certainly its devastation has been etched in the minds of the populace for the rest of their lives. Ordinances have been passed since then restricting structures and permanent dwellings inside the flood plain. Campgrounds and R.V. Parks are regulated as to their months of operations – November through April being closed periods.

Much worse than the 1955 flood, the crest of the flood in 1964 swept away everything in its flow. In the words of Jack Morris, "Even photos will never show the true story here."

Gone were many businesses in the town of Klamath. From the *Flood Extra Edition* of the *Del Norte Triplicate* on January 1, 1965, the headline and story read: "Flood Damage Set at Forty Million."

"Gone are the Three Sevens, The Bee Hive, Rexall Drugs, Klamath Theater, and Brizzard's. The jail and courthouse are partially there and Vern's Tackle was intact but buried in debris, sand and mud. Miraculously, the big fish sign at Vern's Tackle weathered the flood. Klamath School was also buried under tons of sand, silt and debris."

Many of these businesses and people who lost homes, lost them for the second time in less than 10 years. For many the strain was too much and many simply left the area, moved to town (Crescent City) or had their spirit so crushed that they died shortly after. The flood took its toll on the mental status of many residents.

Most of the resorts were hard hit. Half the road to the Requa Boat Dock was washed out and 30 boats were lost. Panther Creek Lodge lost all of its rental units and most of the boats. The lodge was still there but after being under 7 1/2 feet or more of water it was a real mess. Chinook Trailer Park was covered with silt and had much of its land eaten by the hungry Klamath. Camp Klamath and Ritchie's Motel were a total loss.

In the Klamath Glen and Terwer Valley, the Silver Dollar Resort suffered no damage at all, although the water was two feet up on the gas pumps and the flood left the outside covered with debris. Duffy's had one big cabin out but was altogether not too bad off. Glen Port was all but destroyed. Roy Rook's Camp at Terwer lost about a fourth of its trailer spaces and was covered with silt but according to quotes by Roy

Rook in the *Del Norte Triplicate* January 1, 1965: "I'll be back in business by summer!"

The Glen Trailer Park and the Riffles were stripped clean and lost three to four feet of soil, with no chance of rebuilding any permanent structures on either again.

Throughout the state, highways and bridges were hardest hit by the 1964 flood. It was not exclusive to the Klamath and the same destruction was happening on the Eel and Smith rivers. The Douglas Memorial Bridge was no exception and succumbed to the fears of engineers as it was destroyed by the accumulation of giant redwoods and stumps combined with the force of the flow. The center spans were wiped out and the north approach completely destroyed. Only the southern approach remained.

All that remains of the Douglas Memorial Bridge after the 1964 flood. George Burdick photo

The homes in the Glen were lost again and only a few could be repaired. Many yards were buried in silt that was four to five feet deep in some spots. The Federal Government stepped in with flood relief, and the Army Corps of Engineers cleaned the silt from many of the lots.

Upriver the entire flat at McCoveys was gone and there was no sign of the big orchard that had been there. All of the homes at Cleveland Riffle were gone. Mr. Boyd's house, dairy and most of his land was washed away. In the Glen a large redwood stump (it's still there today) lay in a gravel bed with the initials of the Boyd children upon it.

Fletcher's cabin site was covered with logs and no building remained. At Ah Pah the water reached the eaves of the new house and the Orchard (planted by Luther Burbank, see Chapter 4) was under several feet of silt. The old Ward cabin was gone. Seeley Griffin's house cracked and was off its foundation, but was still there, barely!

On the Reservation, the land was stripped of vegetation and none of the homes remained.

One story told of a house which floated out the Klamath with some poor soul stranded atop the roof. As with many stories, I found no documentation in area newspapers, but feel this one is worth the mention. Fact or fiction? I do not know.

The U.S. Army's Fourth Engineers Battalion from Fort Lewis, Washington was transferred to the Klamath River to erect a cable and raft system for crossing the river by motor vehicle.

Ironically, I was 16 years old at the time and one of my first solo driving adventures was to tour the state – gawking like the school boy I was at the tragedy around me. I'll always remember sleeping overnight in the back seat of my Chrysler New Yorker (yes, Mr. Snider, Sally was there!), waiting for the barge to ferry us over the Klamath. I'll also remember the tremendous amount of silt that covered everything. Houses were simply buried in mud!

The Morris Family again was victimized by the flood as were many but a letter written by Jack Morris after the second experience set the tone and the feelings of many at that time. The remaining two buildings left at Blue Creek Lodge were gone, their house in the Glen had gaping holes and Jack wrote, "I've tried to write before but somehow I just can't seem to get my mind to function!"

Quiet Before The Flood

There has not been another flood of real consequence in the last 24 years on the Klamath River. Today in 1989, there is a noticed relaxing of the lessons past floods have taught residents time and time again. More and more buildings, expansion of resorts, and improvements to land inside the flood plain can be seen. As sure as time ticks its weary beat upon your clock; as positive as the winter rains of the north coast; as absolutely as history is sure to repeat itself, is the cycle of floods that come raging down the Klamath River.

3 The Fish

Historically, the Chinook salmon (*Orcorhynchus tshawytscha*) has been the most important of the many anadromous species that inhabit the Klamath River. (Chinook can also be referred to as "king salmon.") Ranking number one with sport and commercial fishermen throughout the river, it is the Chinook species of the salmonidae family people refer to when they say salmon. Anadromous, the Chinook salmon appears silver-blue with a white belly as it enters the mouth of the Klamath. With each proceeding day in fresh water, the females turn a bit darker and the males a crimson red. The jaws and teeth of the males become exaggerated and scales are absorbed, leaving the once shiny salmon with a dull appearance.

Chinook salmon spawn in most of the tributaries of the Klamath. They look for smooth gravel, usually one to six inches in diameter. Eggs take from 30 to 60 days to become fry depending on water temperature. (Warmer water means a quicker hatch.) Downstream migration usually occurs about four to five months later in the high water flow of the spring runoff. Most Klamath River Chinook salmon mature at three or four years of age. An average four year old Klamath Chinook is 31 inches in length and about 15 pounds in weight. Large numbers of male salmon return at two years of age, these are referred to as "jacks" usually weighing 2 to 5 pounds, and are less than 20 inches in length.

Spring Salmon

In the late 1800s and the early 1900s the largest run of Chinook on the Klamath occurred in the spring during the months of June and July. Declining water flows, decreased habitat due to upriver dams and increased summer water temperatures have depleted the spring salmon run throughout the Klamath River. In the 1970s and early 1980s the spring run became almost nonexistent, but rebuilding efforts mostly by the Lewiston Hatchery on the Trinity River have been responsible for the best spring Chinook fishing in over 30 years during 1987 and 1988. Though the large populations, estimated at 40 to 50 thousand, are hatchery fish there are still a few isolated wild populations, like the small run that spawns in Wolley Creek, a tributary of the Salmon River.

Fall Run

In recent years it has been the fall run which has aroused the interest of netters and anglers who fish the Klamath River. Though average weight of these fish is only 10 to 20 pounds, some very large "kings" are taken every year. Ed Hughes who has both guided and commercially netted for the canneries at the mouth for the better part of this century said the largest salmon he ever saw on the Klamath was a 78 pound male he helped to weigh sometime in the 1930s. The past two years, 1986 and 1987, have had astonishing runs when compared to the disastrous numbers of the late 1970s and early 1980s. Rebuilding efforts by state and federal fisheries as well as cutbacks on the user groups and most importantly the lower salmon quota given to the ocean troll for harvest has caused a turnaround in fishing on the Klamath River. In 1985 there were 59,300 fall-run spawners that entered the Klamath River. In 1986 and 1987, 186.3 and 199 thousand adult fall Chinook salmon entered the Klamath! It has never been so obvious where our fish were being caught, as the past two years of cutbacks in the ocean troll have shown.

The Silver Salmon

In California, the official name is silver salmon, but in most other areas it is commonly known as coho salmon, (*Oncorhynchus kisutch*). The average weight of a silver on its spawning migration in the Klamath River is 7 to 12 pounds and fish over 15 are rare. The California angling record is a 22-pound fish taken from a small stream, Papermill Creek in Marin County, January, 1959. Though very silver blue when they enter the river, spawning females appear bronze and males become deep red.

George Caldwell proudly displays a 12 pound male silver salmon caught in October on the Klamath River. George Burdick photo

Silvers enter the river later than the Chinook and spend less time in the river. They usually enter the Klamath in October shortly before spawning. Almost all Klamath silver salmon mature at three years of age and at about 70 centimeters. Most of the present silver salmon population on the Klamath River are hatchery reared at Iron Gate and Lewiston hatcheries.

In October of 1987, the lower Klamath was full of silvers rolling and schooling in the pools. It was an extremely large run and numbered an estimated 23,000 fish.

Steelhead

Simply called a steelhead, *Salmo gairdneri irideus* truly is a sea-run rainbow trout. Entering the river with a beautiful steel blue back above shiny silver sides and snowy white belly, steelhead go through a striking color change during their migration upstream. Upriver the steelhead takes on the look of a normal river-bound rainbow trout, with an olive-green back and red slash along its entire lateral line.

There are two distinct runs of steelhead on the Klamath known as the summer and winter run. The basic difference between the two runs is the time they enter the river. The summer steelhead enter the river in the spring and summer and spend the entire summer waiting until late winter/early spring of the following year to spawn. They move through the lower river at their own pace knowing no spawning urgency, waiting in deep holes or at the mouths of cooler streams. Summer steelhead populations on the Klamath are at an all time low and there are no major restocking efforts at the present time. Upriver project F.I.S.H. may improve this situation (see project F.I.S.H. Chapter 6).

Winter steelhead begin to enter the Klamath in the fall and continue to run until March or April. This run of steelhead is more urgent in its migration and fish reaching the headwaters usually begin spawning immediately.

Steelhead reach the headwaters of virtually every accessible stream in the Klamath River system for their spawning ritual. Unlike Pacific salmon, steelhead do not necessarily die after spawning. Fish that spawn two or three times are not uncommon, though four time spawners are considered rare. Klamath River steelhead spawn on a consecutive basis, that is every year. A first time spawner will average 18 to 20 inches. A second run fish 21 to 25 inches; third time spawners achieving a length of 27 to 29 inches, and averaging about 8 to 10 pounds in weight.

Burney Knoke with a steelhead. This 12-pound mint bright fish started the morning's fishing October 18, 1987 with George Burdick serving as guide. George Burdick photo

Scale Analysis

Studies done on the Klamath River have revealed much about the life histories of the river's steelhead populations. Unlike juvenile Chinook that migrate within months of hatching, steelhead juveniles spend two years in the river system before they make their downstream migration. Scale analysis shows that 90 percent of Klamath River steelhead, with the exception of Trinity River steelhead, return four to five months later as half pounders. (Note: half-pounders are immature steelhead, usually under 17 inches in length and 1 1/2 pounds in weight, and are not on a true spawning run.) Here is where the major difference in life histories of the rivers' steelhead takes an interesting twist. Trinity River steelhead scale samples have shown that only 25 percent of the Trinity fish enter the river on a half-pounder run. This difference between Trinity and all other Klamath River steelhead creates larger steelhead bound for the Trinity. Skipping the half-pounder run, Trinity steelhead remain in the ocean during that year and experience a faster rate of growth and a larger adult size both in length and weight. Studies show fresh water growth rates for Klamath River steelhead to be about 1 inch annually compared with 6.5 inches in the ocean. This makes it easy to understand why the majority of large Klamath steelhead are caught below Weitchpec, the mouth of the Trinity, or in the Trinity River itself.

Sea-Run Brown Trout

The Trinity River also has a small run of sea-run brown trout (*Salmo trutta linnasus*) whose ancestors were imported from Loch Leven in Scotland. In the British Isles they are referred to as "sea-trout." Fresh sea-run browns do not necessarily show any of the yellow or red of a stream-bound brown and can be easily mistaken for steelhead in the lower river. (In seven years fishing the lower river, I've caught one sea-run brown and released it almost thinking it was a steelhead before I caught sight of a subtle difference – the lack of a longitudinal red stripe found in most steelhead.)

The majority of fishing for brown trout, some of which are resident as well as sea-run occurs on the Trinity River. Juvenile brown trout spend two years in the river before migrating to sea, while some brown remain in or near the estuary not straying far from the river.

Coastal Cutthroat Trout

Salmo Clarki Clarki does not migrate up the Klamath River very far and spends much of its time in the estuary or small streams near the mouth. Not all coastal cutthroat go to sea and they are considered to be optionally anadromous by the Department of Fish and Game. Most cutthroat in the Klamath are 12 to 18 inches and weigh one to three pounds. They are often caught but seldom pursued by anglers on the Klamath. Those few who fish for them often reap the joy of catching many easily.

Sturgeon

The Klamath River has two species of sturgeon, green and white. Upstream migration usually ends at Ishi Pishi Falls, but one sturgeon tagged at the mouth was recaptured at Happy Camp far above Ishi Pishi Falls. Actual spawning of sturgeon has never been described and little is known about these long lived individuals of the piscatorial world.

Shad

Actually a member of the herring family, shad run in large schools on the Klamath River but are of little importance to anglers. No one has ever developed a consistent fishery for shad in the Klamath. Even the Indian netters throw away the shad caught in their nets and at times the river has plenty of floating shad decomposing in mid-drift.

Eulachon Are "Candle Fish"

Considered as one of the more flavorful of fishes with a rich oily taste, candle fish, a member of the herring family, was sometimes dried and fitted with a wick to give light, hence the name. Dip nets are used to catch them near the mouth of the river and the run of candlefish has long been important to Native Americans living along the lower Klamath River.

Their eggs are laid free-floating over coarse sand. The outer part of the egg is sticky and adheres to the grains of sand securing the eggs. This delicate species has been severely affected by herbicides used in the forest industry.

Pacific Lamprey

Though not a true fish, the lamprey is referred to as an eel by most of the river residents. Slender and eel like it is not an eel but is anadromous and found throughout the entire length of the Klamath River. Their primary importance is for the Indians who snag them as they enter the mouth of the Klamath. Smoked eel is considered a delicacy by many who have tasted it, including yours truly. Carcasses of dead Lamprey have been found as far upriver as the Shasta Racks on the Shasta River 175 miles from the ocean.

Steelhead Habits

What factors prompt steelhead to move? How far do they travel in a day? If you catch them in one hole today, where will they be tomorrow? The Shasta River is a major spawning habitat of the Klamath River drainage. Fish counts are taken at the Shasta Racks, a fish counting station operated by the Department of Fish and Game.

I had the opportunity to work at the weir and kept a daily diary of water temperature, water condition, weather, daily count and my catch record in order to study the movement of steelhead.

The unnatural navigation of the weir itself may have discouraged fish movement, however being there everyday gave me the feeling that if the trap inhibited movement, I would have seen more fish activity near the weir without any fish passing through the counter. The comparison of count and my catch gave me a clear idea of when I was fishing empty waters. The best of angling skills can't catch steelhead when nobody's home.

Water temperature seems to have the greatest influence in relation to steelhead movement. From November through February, the water temperature on the Shasta River ranged from 34 to 53 degrees. There was zero fish movement until the water warmed to at least 38 degrees.

In winter weather, a warm rain is needed to bring water temperatures up into the 50s. This usually roiled the water and put the steelhead on the move. During very high, muddy water periods, the most steelhead passed through the counter. When the water was clearing after the rain but still warm, I had the best fishing success.

The weather also played a great part in my catch success. The onset of a low pressure system would put the fish off the bite. It seemed that as soon as the front edge of the storm passed and it was raining, I'd have good results.

There are many opinions about how far steelhead travel in a day. It seems that there isn't any set distance and steelhead tagged the same day at the mouth of the Klamath River have arrived at the Shasta Racks (175 river miles upstream) as much as 74 days apart. Why the time difference? That is the beauty of a steelhead that does not travel in the frantic migrational footsteps of its cousin, the salmon. It was a tremendous advantage working at the weir and learning about the habits and movement of steelhead. It has increased my steelheading success immeasurably.

4 Legends, Lodges And Guides

In the development of angling on the Klamath River, it was our predecessors that refined the techniques we use today. The Klamath River has been an important contributor both in salmon and steelhead fishing tactics and tackle. This includes the pioneering of many fly patterns and the invention of much of the terminal tackle still used on the river today. The efforts and talents of these important people should not go unnoticed. The skills they have passed on to future generations of anglers should be praised. We are all following in the path they set before us, standing in the same riffles and even upon the same rocks. Klamath River history is rich in the accomplishments of its fishermen and women. This is the story of but a few of the many who have made the fishing world richer for all those that follow.

O-Meg-Waw is an Indian word meaning, big river.

The Blessing

Indians who first lived at the mouth of the Klamath River had a yearly ritual they performed to bless the salmon that found their way back to the Klamath. As the first fish entered the river, the Yuroks would allow a few to pass, then a designated member of the clan would wrestle a Chinook from the river's mouth and quickly carry it across the beach and up the hill that overlooks the river. Here it would be offered to the four corners of the world. (They believed that the world was square.) Then the salmon was cut into pieces and returned to the river from which it came. After this was done, the rest of the Yuroks could begin fishing. In these early times of Indian lore, it was said to be forbidden to eat salmon on the beach that today is the site of Dad's Camp.

No One's Fish

Sometime in the 1980s there was a curious affair that happened at the mouth of the Klamath. A particularly large salmon was hooked and fought by an elderly man helped by his wife who netted the fish just as the small boat went ker-thunk against the sandy beach. The man slumped forward bent at the waist and his wife realized that something was wrong. Her husband had died from heart failure while he had fought that fish. As the wife rushed to the hospital with her husband, the salmon lay forgotten in the bottom of the boat. The boat was returned to the campground with the fish still left in the boat. Try as they would, the owners of the resort could not find anyone who would take that fish. Truly a story of a man who had died with a fish on it would always be his fish, because it was certainly no one's salmon now.

Bigfoot

The Klamath River and the Trinity Alps are in the heart of Bigfoot country. Over the course of the last 20 years or more there have been several sightings. Including one as recently as 1988, when Bigfoot was seen by a motorist on a state highway. In the town of Klamath near the frontage road, on the south end of what little town remains, there is a marked grave that denotes Bigfoot's passing. Though this grave is a local joke, there are many people who believe in the legend of Bigfoot here in Klamath Country.

Legend Of The First Fly Fisher

Many years ago, along the banks of one of our great rivers, there stood a wary angler. One whose very existence depended upon the ability to catch enough fish to survive. This particular fly fisher ate only fish and the skill with which the finny creatures were enticed to the surface by his offerings are a credit to his breed.

The great blue heron cocks a wary eye to good holding water, wades in, plucks a feather from its breast and cranes its neck far upstream dropping the delicate and buoyant "insect" upon the water. Following it downstream with watchful eyes, the beak ever ready to grab any tempted fish with a powerful stab. So effective is the blue heron as a fly fisher that its pelts of feathers became some of the most prized by fly tiers. Hunted almost to the point of extinction, the great blue heron was placed on the endangered species list and has made a marked comeback. It is unlawful to use or possess blue heron pelts although many old timers still have a fly or two tied with blue heron, the first fly fisher.

Dad's Camp

Owned since the 1900s by the Williams family, Dad's Camp sits on the beach at the mouth of the Klamath River. Its timeless nature, billed as the "eighth wonder of the world" makes every journey to the mouth of the river a special experience. Dynamic in nature, the activity of river and the sea as well as a total predator environment heighten the senses when at the mouth.

Charlie Williams was the patriarch of the family and with his wife Annie, ran the longhouse at the end of the stage route from Trinidad. The longhouse was used by the stage's passengers and had several rooms. It boasted a huge social room with a grand fireplace that warmed many a weary traveler after the long journey up the coast from Trinidad and Eureka.

In 1892, the U.S. Government required homesteaders to fence all lands. Unable to fence his entire homestead, Charlie Williams fenced in the area nearest the sea claiming it for all time for the Williams family. He also notified the government that he was willing to relinquish the rest of his land. This released land later became the Fortain Ranch. This was at a time when California was yet to become a state.

Timm Williams was proud to be "Chief Lightfoot," the living mascot of the Stanfor University Indians.

Sometime in 1898, a young Greek woman named Sofia Simmons came by stage to the longhouse. She made a living by selling scissors, tape, bits of cloth and other things people in the isolated areas of California couldn't buy. She was also eight months pregnant. She gave birth to a young boy named Harry and stayed at the longhouse working for another three weeks. She then abandoned the child, saying only that she would return for him when she could. Being childless,

Charlie and Annie grew quite fond of the boy and adopted him as their own son. The Williams, both Yurok Indians, raised their Greek son, Harry. For all real purposes, he was Indian except for the blood that flowed through his veins. Harry took to telling people that he was Indian. The woman, Sophia returned 17 years later, but her son was content in his wondrous home at the mouth of the Klamath River. Charlie died in 1946 leaving all to his adopted son, Harry Williams.

Harry married a Yurok woman, Ethel Marie Jones and ran Dad's Camp for many years. In the 1930s there were two camps, one on the hill overlooking the mouth and a beach camp where the present camp is located. They had three sons, Charlie, Desmond (Juke) and Timm. All three guided tourists for Chinook salmon at the mouth. The family was proud of its spinner fishing and felt that if only one fish were caught on a spinner during the day it would be by one of them. The Williams boys rowed the mouth fishing with spinners, but there were also three daughters: Vivian, Dorthy and Fawn. Vivian followed her mother's lead of baking some of the best blackberry pies Klamath has ever known. Harry Williams died in 1964.

Timm Williams was certainly one of the most famous figures in Klamath and no doubt the most famous Yurok Indian. Timm met an untimely death in a car accident in 1988 and is buried in the family burial site overlooking the mouth of the Klamath. Timm served as Prince Lightfoot, the living mascot of the Stanford University Indians for 21 years from 1951 through 1972. Then the team changed its name to the Stanford Cardinals amid growing sensitivity towards American Indians in the 1970s. It is an irony that Timm had used his position at the university to gain admission for many Native Americans at a time when Stanford was a private university. Timm Williams was also pictured in full costume as the centerfold for *Esquire* and his picture also appeared in Life. In addition, he was an artist of some renown and became involved with Indian rights through United Indian Health Services.

People come to Dad's Camp for many reasons, but all are humbled by the magnitude of this campground where the river meets the sea. Dad's Camp is still the place to go for salmon fishing at the mouth of the Klamath. Many shore-casters crowd together to swing 2 to 8 ounces of lead with an accompanying spinner. There are also surf casters who fish for red-tailed perch in the ocean just outside the mouth of the Klamath. In a world all its own, Dad's Camp remains timeless at the mouth of the Klamath River.

Requa Inn

Originally the Pioneer Inn and owned by John Miller, the Requa Inn was moved to its present location in 1895. It was also called the Klamath Inn during its 100 year tenure overlooking the estuary below. Fire ravaged the inn in 1914 as well as many other buildings in the town of Requa. When the inn reopened in 1915, there was a grand ball held June 4th with dancing and music provided by a stringed orchestra. Dancing was free although dinner cost 50 cents that night. The inn was owned by many, including notorious sea captain, William Crone, who sold the inn to Elsie Larson in 1947.

Elsie Larson was quite a woman in the town of Klamath in those wild and woolly days. She began coming to the Klamath at the age of nine, spending summers away from her birthplace in Eureka where she was born in 1903. When Elsie was 16 years old, she began work at a salmon cannery where her brother was the superintendent.

Larson's Cabins alongside Highway 101. Elsie Larson pumping gas for a customer.

She married W. (Walderman) "Baldy" Larson and in 1929 the two began Larson's Cabins, a resort alongside highway 101 and the Klamath River. They ran the cabins, a coffee shop, store and gas station until 1945, and employed many guides, one of whom was Eddie Spott. Sadness however struck the Larson family in 1942, when Baldy was hurt in a cedar mill accident and never recovered, dying in the local hospital two days later.

Shortly after, Elsie purchased the Requa Inn and owning such a grand establishment gave her the position of being one of the most desirable women in town. She was known during this period to have danced "on every bar in Klamath." But says Elsie, these stories were "not true."

"I never danced on the bar at the Klamath Club, because I was too tall to fit between the bar top and the ceiling," said Elsie with a mischievous smile. Elsie was also Del Norte County's first skinny dipper and would take many a midnight swim in the estuary below the Requa Inn. One day a tourist came to the inn saying he had seen a mermaid in the river the night before. That same night when Elsie went for a swim, there he was. Says Elsie, "that S.O.B. had a flashlight."

Elsie Larson remarried in 1951 to Patrick Gussin, although many people still refer to this grand lady as a Larson. Elsie ran the inn for 25 years and also started a second business, the Requa Boat Docks. Over 200 boats were owned by Requa Docks and they employed 20 guides during its height of popularity.

The boats themselves were made by an Italian man named Tony Garony. He built not only the boats for the lodge, but many of the wooden rowboats used by the guides for fishing at the mouth of the Klamath, as well as the 150 boats for Shorty Conner's Camp.

Many famous figures stayed at the inn and because of its beauty, location and of course the fishing, the Requa Inn attracted many of the movers and shakers during its reign as "The Place To Go" on the Klamath River. Radio, TV and movie stars as well as sports figures stayed at the inn. Zane Grey stayed at the inn during his visits to fish the mouth. Two of the best and most well known guides, Jack "The Swede" Husberg and Ed Hughes worked for the inn and took many of these people salmon fishing. A 66-pound salmon was the largest recorded at Requa Inn.

During the 1955 flood, Requa Inn was used to house many of the homeless victims of the Klamath River's fury. For about three months, 100 or more people stayed at the inn. School was also held there and it was perhaps the only time in history that the students entered the "schoolhouse" through a cocktail lounge.

Elsie sold the inn to her son-in-law, Norman Bush in 1971 and there were several other owners before it was closed for about two years. In its over 100 years of operation the inn has been closed twice for a total of three years. It now has been reopened by the current owners, Paul and Donna Hamby.

Panther Creek Lodge

Panther Creek is the largest stream entering the Klamath River estuary and on its banks Vance Farmer built Panther Creek Lodge. Originally a two story building, an additional wing of cabins was added later. The lodge had a boat ramp in the mouth of the creek and docks on the banks of the river. During the 1964 flood, the cabins were destroyed and there was water in the second floor of the main lodge. It was then that the new owner, Don Duvol, was informed by the Army Corps of Engineers that they would not build the rip rap for future flood protection until all livable structures inside the flood plain were torn down. It was with great reluctance that Don burned the lodge to the ground.

Panther Creek has been one of the central lodges for mouth fishermen and a coordinating spot for guides. Many Indian and white guides worked for both Vance Farmer and Don Duvol. Don has been active in the Klamath Chamber of Commerce as well as the Klamath River Basin Task Force. The lodge is gone, but an R.V. park remains and Panther Creek anglers still catch many of the large salmon at the mouth of the Klamath, including the salmon that hangs on the wall of the Klamath post office.

The First Lodge At Blue Creek

Long about 1923, Elmer and Rose Miles ran a fishing lodge just downstream from the mouth of Blue Creek on the Klamath River. It was one of

An old photo of Panther Creek Lodge. Del Norte Historical Society photo

the first lodges in the remote area upstream from the town of Klamath. Accessed only by river traffic, the lodge offered a near wilderness fishing experience in those pioneering times of angling. Fishing was for the most limited to bait and lures and the river was very productive for salmon and steelhead.

The lodge boasted clients from as far away as England and was very popular with San Franciscans who made up the majority of the guests. Some of those who fished at Blue Creek Lodge included San Franciscan, Bret Harte, a famous writer of this period and also President Herbert Hoover who frequented many areas of the Klamath River. Blue Creek Lodge used Indian guides who rowed the clients in old Boyd double enders. Elmer and Rose also had a son, Bob who was about five years old at the time. Memories are thin, but Bob had several pictures of the lodge his parents ran. As so many before and after, the lodge met an untimely end when the great flood of 1927 washed it and the very earth it was built upon away into the torrent the Klamath River knows at flood stage. Bob Miles returns to the Klamath every season and in 1967 his nephew, Glen Miles, caught a 17 pound 11 ounce steelhead on Waukel Riffle. This fish won the 1967 Garcia Rod and Reel photo contest.

Blue Creek Lodge

One lodge stands out on the lower Klamath River in its historical importance to the development of fly fishing and fly tying. Blue Creek Lodge was operated from 1936 through 1955 when it was ravaged by the floodwaters of Christmas Eve. The lodge was located just downstream and across the river from Blue Creek on land bought from Mills College. There Oakland born Jack Morris and his wife Mable ran the lodge, boated the river, tied flies and in time Jack became known as "Blue Creek Jack." The lodge once consisted of 30 or more cabins, a kitchen, laundry and a main lodge. Now absolutely no trace remains of this once busy resort.

Moving to Klamath, Jack's entire family followed and his father and mother also came along. At this point, Jack's sister followed too saying: "If you think I'll stay in the city you're crazy." Along the river "Pop" Morris and his son "Blue Creek" Jack plied the river with flies for summer-run steelhead and were two of the pioneers in the growing sport of catching steelhead on the fly. In fact almost all the fishing done from Blue Creek Lodge was fly fishing in June and July. There were of course occasional egg dunkers and hardware salesmen at the lodge but they always received a hard time from the fly purists that were the regular guests. By nature, though, Blue Creek Lodge was a fly fishing lodge and is responsible for the fame that Blue Creek developed as one of the best fly fishing areas on theKlamath River.

Fly developments at the lodge were to the credit of Bug Bishop and Mable Morris. They also carried many flies tied by a baker from Eureka, Lloyd Silvius, who gained later fame as a tier and originator of the Brindal Bug. At first the fly of choice was the Thor, a pattern originated by Jim Pray in 1934, but variations developed and the Bug Special as well as the Blue Creek Special became the two favorites used at the lodge. The flies as described to me by Bug Bishop were of "yellow chenille body with bucktail tied in and a red tail, they were underdressed and understated and the only real difference between the two was the addition of a grizzly hackle on the Bug Special."

At the suggestion of Jerome Rosefield, the founder of Skippy Peanut Butter, Mable Morris wound wire around the shank of the hooks on the next dozen Blue Creek Specials to produce a weighted version of the fly. This early 1940 venture into casting and fishing weighted flies proved successful and the idea spread among California fly tiers and added to the growing fame of Blue Creek Lodge.

The lodge used a boat that was dug out from a single redwood log 24 feet in length and 6 foot in beam. The boat was to gain fame in *Ripleys Believe It Or Not* in 1977 for hauling supplies and passengers over 48,000 miles on the Klamath River. This was the same boat used a decade earlier by Frank Ryerson for commercial hauling on the Klamath. Trips in this dugout took 45 minutes to go from town to the lodge about 10 miles upriver.

Jack Morris was one of the first to attempt to preserve the integrity of the river and tried to establish a green belt 200 yards wide on each side of the river free from logging. He also tried to have the rafts of logs that were towed down the river banned and fought against the prop washing (sediment) of channels by tugs. Upstream mining was also a problem in those days and until the mines shut down, every July, most of the June fishing was done along the edges of the muddy river or in the clear water discharges of feeder streams.

A young boy of eight and his seven-pound steelhead held by guide Brad Throgmorton. Steve Riede photo

Jack Morris of Blue Creek Lodge offers food and comfort to Oscar Taylor and Slim Coates near Blue Creek. Their light 4 h.p. engine made the last 180 miles with only the light copper water tubes holding the motor to the frame but won the first Klamath River White Water Dare Devil Race. Del Norte Historical Society photo

Jack and Mable Morris spent 25 years running a lodge in the pioneering times of fly fishing on the Klamath River. Their guests included many famous people and some not so famous. Each and everyone became a friend. A visit to Blue Creek often touched one's heart and an encounter with this beautiful land kept many forever returning to the lovely lodge near Blue Creek. Summers at the lodge included personalities like Vic Bergeron, of Trader Vic's in San Francisco, or philanthropist Doctor Hans Klausman whose wife, Anne, once spent her entire summer planning a strategy for saving San Francisco's cable cars. Aren't we all lucky she was successful!

The great disaster of the 1955 flood washed away Jack and Mable's resort and totally destroyed all but two of the cabins and a bathroom from Blue Creek Lodge. It also destroyed Jack and Mable's home in Klamath Glen. Hurt but not broken, Jack and Mable moved north on the redwood highway across from the trees of mystery and built the Trees Motel. In 1962, Jack Morris started a jet boat tour upriver named the *Chub II* after his son, and made trips to Roach Creek where the guests would picnic and then return downriver. The boat was piloted by Bert Plukovoy and carried about 40 passengers. There was a second boat, the *Maye-B* piloted by Court Boice, and both jet boats were made by Boice Boats. This was the first jet boat tour and lasted only three years because the Klamath was to know another flood that ended Jack and Mable's intimate relationship with the river.

Nearly nine years to the day after the great Christmas Eve 1955 flood, 1964 proved to be the "flood of 1,000 years" and wiped Klamath from the land it once stood upon. This crushing blow took away the remaining cabins and most of the land on which the lodge had been built. Jack's newsletter after the second flood in less than 10 years was one of near disbelief and almost held an admitted tone of defeat. It expressed the feelings of many for whom the second flood proved too much. Jack wrote, "Dear Friends, I've tried to write before but somehow I just can't seem to get my mind to function. This thing was so much worse than the 1955 flooding and it's so huge of a mess that words cannot describe it!"

During the time that Blue Creek Lodge was open there were two neighboring cabins in the general area. These were the cabins of Bill Olson at Ah Pah owned by Sage Land and Lumber Company and the cabin of Colonel Ed Fletcher, an attorney who'd taken the little house at Blue Creek in exchange for handling the affairsof the Ward estate. Colonel Fletcher was famous throughout California for his land acquisitions in lieu of payment. Bill Olson, however was a handicapped logger who became caretaker of the cabin at Ah Pah. He often exchanged summer lodging with city refugees seeking the escape and solitude of the Klamath River for work in his organic garden. One of his summer workers was young Luther Burbank who planted an orchard for Bill Olson while he stayed there. The orchard remains there even today as it was planted on high ground and survived the great floods. Luthor Burbank was one of our country's leading horticulturists and developed the nectarine fruit tree. He spent quite a bit of time on the Klamath River.

Vern's Tackle

Vern and Ann Flachsman

Along about 1912, a young Swiss immigrant came to the Klamath River. His name was Vern Flachsman and he came to the Klamath aboard the steamer *Coaster* captained by the notorious sea captain William Crone. Vern worked at first as a cook in Requa Inn before fire destroyed the inn. Then the frugal and farsighted Mr. Flachsman built his own store in Requa where he sold groceries, hardware and fishing tackle. The store also had the first soda fountain in the area and was a favorite among local youngsters.

He later moved to Klamath, where he ran Vern's Tackle for 40 years. This thoughtful, innovative man was responsible for many of the systems of rigging and spinner design to be used on the Klamath River. His store flourished and was the place to go in Klamath. Vern once advised a very young Ray Benner to "let your spinner rest a moment when it hits the bottom before you pick it back up again." His friendly attitude,

The original jet boat tours were started by Jack and Mable Morris. Here the Chub II built by Boice Boats passes Moores Rock about 25 miles up the Klamath River. Blue Creek Lodge photo

helpful nature and boundless desire to design anything he could to make fishing more efficient led Vern to many of the inventions and innovations for which he is given credit. Vern is also remembered for always having a spare jar of salmon eggs to give to a restless child. He kept the local children in bait without charge.

Throughout the West, there has been an item in the fishing world which has long been referred to as the "Klamath Cinch" invented by Vern Flachsman. It is the surgical tubing attached to a swivel, either barrel or three way, and used to hold your pencil lead when drift fishing. The Klamath Cinch is still one of the most popular methods for securing pencil lead when drift fishing.

Vern and Ann Flachsman made some of the best spinner patterns ever used at the mouth of the Klamath. The monofilament spreader for spinners using heavy line instead of wire was an invention of Vern's. He also developed a system for making spinners that started the wire in a figure eight instead of the simple loop. This held the hook firm and it would not bend from side to side. Ann Flachsman taught Ron Benedict how to make their spinner patterns when they sold the remains of the tackle shop to Ron and his father Mike in 1971. As Ron says, "Ann took me to spinner school several nights."

The original wooden building that Vern's Tackle was located in washed away in the 1955 flood. Vern then built a concrete building that was said to be flood proof, but the 1964 flood took that claim to its limits. Though it was one of only a couple of buildings left standing, Vern's Tackle was awash with silt and debris. Vern and Ann then worked in a small shop north of Klamath until failing health caused them to leave the area. They moved to Sacramento in 1976 and have since passed away.

Kutzkey Lodge

Three generations of Kutzkeys have used their skill as anglers to ply their trade upon the Klamath River. The eldest of the Kutzkeys, Al, was one of the best known guides on the Klamath River. Famous for his skill as an oarsman and his craft at taking steelhead, Al was perhaps most impressive because of the volume of knowledge he possessed. Self educated and willing to read any and every book he could get his hands on, Al was a student of ecology, self taught in geology, philosophy and biology. The one time Colorado River trapper came to the Klamath in the 1950s and settled near Hornbrook on the upper Klamath River.

As the acknowledged master of drift fishing, Al referred to the Klamath as his "liquid love." An outing with Al would often be a combination lecture on any subject that crossed his mind while steelhead fishing through stretches of white water and boulders with Al deftly sliding the boat in and out of currents.

"Lines out," and Al would drop the boat into every piece of holding water on the river. It was known fact that Al knew every piece of holding water from Hornbrook to Somes Bar and some stretches below Ishi Pishi Falls, too. Al was at home on the river and one with the oars that powered his boat. A few rare people are separate from others and feel the river in their blood, of these people it is said, "the river flows through them." Al Kutzkey was such a man.

A nice steelhead caught on Al Kutzkey's favorite yellow Hot Shot. Kutzkey Lodge photo

Born in Portland, Oregon on February 12th, 1912, Al traveled throughout the West and at 19 made a solo journey from Green River, Wyoming to the Mexican border traveling down the Green and Colorado rivers by boat.

Tim Kutzkey in the Ikes riffle. Kutzkey Lodge photo

Kutzkey Lodge, located in Siskiyou County, was started in December of 1954, and the Kutzkeys pioneered drift fishing in the upper river. Al Kutzkey was one of the people chosen by Eddie Pope to field test and help in the design of the Hot Shot lure. Al became the king of plugs and perfected the art of using every current, seam and flow to present the wobbling vibration of the Hot Shot to aggressive steelhead. On the upper river, yellow became Al's color of choice and many of his fish were caught on yellow Hot Shots. Al also helped to develop the Frisky Fly and field tested many other not so successful ideas for the tackle companies of the era.

Al fished many famous people out of the lodge, among them, astronauts Buzz Aldrin and Walter Schirra, Melbourne Stone (Gunsmoke's "Doc"), George Peppard and California newspaper and radio personalities. One frequent description of Al and his boat that appeared in every article about him was, "Al was always in appearance casual to say the least, his personal fishing gear was in a constant state of disarray and the boat well, lets just say unkept." This same description was used in *Field and Stream*, *Outdoor Life* and by several major newspaper reporters from the Bay area. But, in spite of it all, each and everyone enjoyed their time in Al's boat as "fishing with the master."

Al Kutzkey was president of Save the Klamath, Inc., the Association of Chambers of Commerce of Siskiyou County and of Shasta Cascade Wonderland Association. In 1980 he was inducted into the Fishing Hall of Fame and was accredited with perfecting the drift boat and Hot Shot lure system.

Al lived his life the way he wanted, right to the very end. Diagnosed as having a coronary problem and after having suffered several mild attacks, Al Kutzkey refused to be admitted to the hospital. For months he told everyone he was a "walking time bomb" and as is just and fair, Al Kutzkey passed away on the Klamath River in the drift boat he loved, with his son Tim at the oars. Al lived his way and his passing was something that romantic tales of adventure are made of.

Tim Kutzkey was born February 18, 1943 and following in his father's oarstrokes, Tim became a master oarsman surpassing even the skill of his father. Tim began to row commercially as a

A young Tim Kutzkey rows white water below Bluff Creek. Kutzkey Lodge photo

guide in 1959 and was the first to row the upper Sacramento River in a drift boat. He is also one of the few who have rowed the treacherous South Fork of the Smith River.

Tim is also an excellent fisherman and I've personally seen many days when Tim's boat was the only one to bring in a fish, or the only boat to limit. Tim also inherited the innovative nature of his father and should be credited with the idea of using the Luhr Jensen Jet Planer as a sliding affair and perfected its rigging. He suggested breaking off the tab that normally has your leader tied to it and clipping the adjustable swivel to a free sliding snap swivel with a barrel swivel in between your main line and leader. This allows the plane to slide and not constantly fight the fish. It is this method of "plane fishing" that is popular on Alaska's Kenai River.

Albert Kutzkey with a 30 pound salmon caught 175 miles from the ocean in the upper Klamath River. Kutzkey Lodge photo

Tim's son Albert, born in 1962, began rowing as a 10 year old. On days Tim would limit the clients between the upriver launch and the lodge, an excited Albert would get to row the boat down to the truck with his dad. Albert began guiding at 14 and had the customers drive the truck to and from fishing and the lodge. Though he is an experienced guide now, Albert plans to become a school teacher. Albert is a third generation guide and it will be a loss to the guiding community when the last Kutzkey leaves the Klamath River that they've all worked so long. These days, Tim is also pursuing other goals and has a body and paint shop in Red Bluff, California.

The Kutzkey's summer camp at Green Riffle near Somes Bar should also be mentioned. In this camp, Al and Tim caught many sturgeon in the deep holes below the big dikes. They also rowed the lower Trinity for sea-run browns and summer-run steelhead.

Beaver Creek Lodge

This one-time private retreat built in the 1950s by Mr. Barker withstood both of the floods in 1955 and 1964 that washed away so many of the river's lodges. Bill and Lela Claypole bought the house and cabins from Frank Klinger in 1971 and ran a quality lodge until they sold it in 1983.

Located on the upper Klamath River, about three miles upstream from Beaver Creek, the lodge was almost exclusively a steelhead fishing lodge with winter steelhead the quarry. Almost all of the fishing was done using a drift boat to float the white water found in this portion of the Klamath. Bill Claypole owned one of the first aluminum drift boats on the upper river; it was built by Glen Wooldridge and had wooden gunnels.

Some nice steelhead for two anglers taken in 1972. Beaver Creek Lodge photo

The lodge gained much of its legendary fame through promotions done by San Francisco-based writers and radio personalities. Fishing at the lodge by writers like Ed Neal of *Western Outdoor News*, Harlen Bartlett of the *Oakland Tribune* and Jim Freeman from the *San Francisco Chronicle*, who spent a week at Beaver Creek Lodge making one of the early fishing videos, helped the lodge gain notoriety. Radio talk show host Frank Dill, "The Morning Man" of KNBR, and Bill Dwyer, the station manager, fished at Beaver Creek and surprised Bill by providing a free blurb on the morning radio show. "There was something really exciting about being wished luck and spoken to from San Francisco while rowing down the Klamath River," says Bill.

Orville and Dolly Riersgaurd on their anniversary fishing trip, a present from Bill Claypole. Beaver Creek Lodge photo

Bill and Lela Claypole ran a quality resort for 12 years on the upper river. They gave many young guides some of their first opportunities in the industry. Among these guides was their own son Bob Claypole who is still guiding in the area today. Other guides who began at Beaver Creek Lodge were Dale Lacky, Steve Riede, Hal Borg and Roy Barnes. In its peak years, 1980 to 1983, the lodge ran five boats a day. Bill Claypole began guiding in 1969 when he owned the Oaks Trailer Park. Bill was a retired real estate developer prior to moving to Siskiyou County.

John Reginato of the Shasta Cascade Wonderland Association, a recreation group, was very helpful in promoting Beaver Creek Lodge and fished with Bill many times. Don Martin wrote articles about Beaver Creek Lodge and the Klamath River that appeared in *Motorland*, the travel magazine put out by Triple A. There was a normal routine many of the writers followed and that was to hire Al Kutzkey out of Hornbrook, drop downriver to fish out of Beaver Creek Lodge with Bill Claypole and then proceed downstream still further to Happy Camp and float the river with Jim Roads. This made for many interesting comparisons of the guides and their services by the writers.

Bill tells a story about a day to remember when he and Hal Borg launched at Presido Bar about 15 minutes behind Jim Proctor, one of the best Indian guides. In a drift boat there is often an advantage to be gained by staying ahead of the other boats and being the first boat to fish each run. Jim Proctor got caught up in this hurry up and stay ahead syndrome and beat Bob and Hal to every hole all morning long. At lunch all three boats, Bob's, Hal's and Jim's beached at the same gravel bar. Jim, hands in his pockets walked over to Bill and Hal grumbling because he didn't have a fish in the boat. That's when Bill and Hal showed him the four limits of 20 nice steelhead, (when the limit was 5 fish). Jim threw up his hands, got his people back in the boat and rowed down river muttering and shaking his head.

Bill Claypole and Hal Borg on the Ti Bar run, October, 1974, back when the steelhead limit was five fish per day. Beaver Creek Lodge photo

Indian guide Eddie Spott and a happy customer on the Klamath River in 1930. Mable Morris photo

Jim Roads

Jim fished from his headquarters in Happy Camp during the 1950s and 1960s. As an ex-logger, Jim took to guiding as a way to provide income during the winter when most jobs in the woods shut down. Jim first rowed a drift boat, but was said to be the first guide to use a jet boat in the Happy Camp area. This was not a popular situation among local anglers who protested vigorously to the Department of Fish and Game.

Jim was an original field tester for Storm Lure Co. and popularized the Wee Wart for catching steelhead on the Klamath. He was a hard working guide who provided every comfort possible for his fishing guests. Jim was famous for the fine lunches his wife Helen would make each night for the day ahead.

As was Al Kutzkey a stubborn man, so is Jim Roads. These two were rivals most of the years they guided, and the two were both headstrong individuals who went their own way and by doing so advanced fishing techniques. Hard headed and set in his ways, Jim Roads refuses (just as did Al Kutzkey) to let the doctors have their way with a developing heart condition.

Jim Roads was the original president of the Klamath River Guides Association and also president of the Klamath Trinity Coalition which reached agreement with the State Water Resources Department to insure that minimum flows are discharged from Iron Gate and Lewiston dams on the Klamath and Trinity rivers during spawning migrations.

Jim also guided on the lower Klamath where he worked from Redwood Rest Resort. He was one of the first to harl flies from a boat and tied very large 1/0 to 2/0 size Brindle Bugs that were very effective for steelhead in fast water riffles.

Jim showed me many tricks running and maintaining my first jet boat, a 14 footer with 20 horsepower, and always stressed less weight to me because of the loss of power experienced when converting to a jet. Jim now lives in Oregon near Medford and summers along the Oregon Coast and in the town of Klamath at the Redwood Rest Resort.

Indian Guides

Indian guides played a big part in fishing for salmon at the mouth of the Klamath River. It was at the mouth that they excelled, fishing spinners and anchovies for Chinook from low sided wooden row boats. Virtually every family had one or more members who rowed tourists and guided fishermen from all over the world. Their skill and fame often caused tourists to prefer going with an Indian Guide to all others. Very few of the Indian guides ventured upriver in early fishing history. One of the first Yuroks to guide in a conventional drift boat on the upper river was Jim Proctor.

Jim was very concerned about the future of the river and was the only Indian member of the Klamath River Guides Association. He worked the mouth in July and August and then moved upriver to guide steelhead fishermen throughout the winter. Jim worked until the 1970s and spent many years in Homer, Alaska. His friendly nature and open mind helped to better the understanding between whites and Indians. Jim Proctor left the Klamath "forever" in 1988 on his way to South America where he planned to find new adventure.

Ron Gensaw, along with most of the Gensaw family, has guided at the mouth but Ron also was one of the fearless competitors of the Klamath White Water Daredevil Race. His friendly nature and open smile make Ron a pleasure to fish with. Ron's black derby hat cocked lightly to the side and his brisk walk make him one of Klamath's most recognizable characters.

Eddie Spott was the son of Robert Spott. Eddie worked for the Requa Inn and later the Requa Docks. As have so many of those who fish the mouth Eddie was claimed by the sea after drowning at the mouth of the Klamath River. Small in size but large in heart, Eddie is remembered by many Klamath anglers. James Brooks was the winner of the Carnegie Medal for bravery. James saved two lives at the mouth of the Klamath River. On August 21, 1930 he rescued Kirby and Floyd Peters from the vicious surf at the mouth of the Klamath. He went to their aid at a time when no one else would dare to attempt the rescue. He was a well known guide and had, on several occasions, gone to the aid of other fishermen at the mouth. Ironically he would drown 19 years later in August, 1949.

Wilford Sanderson was known to all as Sandy. Wilford fished in his distinctive hard hat. This was a necessary safeguard from the heavy weights shore casters would fling, sometimes right into the boat. When Sandy had a fish on everyone knew it by the whooping cry that he used. Fishing spinners and anchovies, Wilford guided for Panther Creek Lodge in the tidewater of the Klamath River.

Guide Sandy Sanderson with two happy customers. Sanderson photo

Sonny Smith Williams, used spinners, "the family pride," to become one of the best salmon fishermen at the mouth of the Klamath River. The number one spinner of choice says Sonny, is the CV-7 by Luhr Jensen. The entire Williams family fished the river but Sonny became the most famous and in fact one of his largest Chinook hangs on the back wall of the Ship Ashore Resort. Sonny Williams, "Indian Guide – Spinner Pride."

There were of course, many other Indian's who "pulled the sticks" at the mouth of the Klamath during its heyday when the fishing was great.

Frank Ryerson

Frank Ryerson resided on the Klamath River near Martin's Ferry and was one of the first to run a commercial boat for hauling commerce on the river. As early as 1923, Ryerson ran a craft for commercial transportation and hauled everything from Indian netters, who worked in the canneries, to a quarter ton load of cherries bound for market. Ryerson was also reported to have hauled five tons of live hogs down the river to Requa. His boat was 24 feet in length with a 6-foot beam hollowed from a single redwood log. It was powered by an Overland four cylinder engine that obtained 32 horsepower and drew 12 inches of water when fully loaded. One of the many large rocks on the Klamath between Johnson's and Martin's ferries is named Ryerson's Rock. It will be there for all time, named for one of Klamath River's boating pioneers.

Ed Hughes

What can be said about a man still guiding at the age of 82! Born in 1906, Ed began fishing the mouth of the Klamath River in 1924 both as a commercial netter and a guide. He was originally paid 10 cents a pound for fish he netted for the canneries. Netting in the morning and guiding tourists in the afternoon, Ed worked hard for his money. Guides in those early days on the Klamath stroked the oars for 10.00 a day. By the 1930s, guides were making 25.00 to 50.00 a day.

Ed's father started one of the first sawmills in Klamath near Hunters Creek and Ed built his house near the present site of Del's Camp. The road there is named Hughes Road for his family. They also had a small camp there called Hughes' Camp. Luther Burbank used to spend a lot of time in Del Norte County discussing horticulture and history with Ed's brother Ralph, who was a local historian of some note. Both Ralph and Ed attended school in Requa.

Ralph Hughes and an unnamed companion with a 43 pound Chinook salmon caught at the mouth of the Klamath River. Ed Hughes photo

Ed guided at the mouth with Jack "The Swede" Husberg and Jack Patapoff, a Russian immigrant. The three became friends and are still talked about by many of the old timers. Jack "The Swede" rowed until he was 88 years old and is one of the historic figures of fishing at the mouth of the Klamath. In the early years the spring run of Chinook was the largest run on the Klamath and the Three Musketeers would row with white bill caps from July until the run was over and then head up to the Smith River and row the mouth there. Ed has always fished in tide water and has rarely ventured upriver.

Ed Hughes has had his share of famous guests to fish with, including Leo Dorsey, Ginger Rogers, Fred McMurray (who hung out with the guides and was a real regular guy), Bill Clothier, who was John Wayne's personal camera man, Amos, of the radio Amos 'n Andy show (but Ed doesn't remember his real name) and Zane Grey. Ed saw the 57-pound Chinook that Zane caught (see Zane Grey) on his own and remembers the time Zane Grey floated down the Klamathwith a Chinese cook. At that time no one would allow a "China Man" in Del Norte County and Zane left a bit perturbed.

The largest salmon Ed ever caught while guiding some 64 years on the Klamath was 43 pounds. Ed did help weigh a 78-pound monster on the Klamath and remembers that the fishermen thought they had a sturgeon until they saw the fish. The day he caught the 43 pounder, he remembers the lady, full of impatience and complaining that she didn't believe there was a damn fish in the river. As Ed turned the boat downriver he saw the line stop and yelled "jerk." When the woman pulled back, she was into a 43-pound Chinook that made her forget her statement and start screaming joyously. Ed recalls a time when silver salmon came into the mouth so thick their leaping and rolling made it look as if it were raining on the water.

Ed ran a trailer park for a time in Klamath but presently lives in Crescent City, California. He still guides, but uses an outboard motor instead of oars. Ed Hughes is one of the original guides on the Klamath River and the son of a true pioneer on the lower river. His silver boat is still part of the daily scene fishing the mouth of the Klamath River.

Al Foss

Born in 1917, Al has been rowing the Klamath River near the town of Orleans since he was 14 years old. Back in 1931 the first boat Al rowed was an old Boyd double ender. The Foss family were some of the original pioneers of northern California and Al's great grandfather owned one of the first sawmills on the Eel River. Al Foss formerly owned the Orleans Hotel and remembers that in the 1964 flood the water was five feet deep in the hotel dining room.

It's hard to get Al to talk about himself. He's more interested in his new effort of spearheading project F.I.S.H.

"We're going to bring back the quality steelhead that were once found in Bluff Creek before the 1964 flood destroyed much of the stream. Bluff Creek used to have some of the biggest and hottest steelhead in the entire Klamath River system; many of them 12 to 15 pounds," explains Al.

Though money is a problem, project F.I.S.H. has hopes for rebuilding a steelhead fishery in mid-river, where the fishing has suffered the most during the last decade.

Al Foss with his fifth steelhead for the day. Gutchen Robb photo

But if you can get Al talking about himself and history, you may learn more about the hydraulic mining that caused early fly fishers to work the edges and schedule their fishing around the weekend closures of the mines. The continual muddy water would finally clear when they shut down the mines during summer low water.

Al told me about the time Bill Conrad came to Orleans to pursue steelhead on the fly and spent the entire time complaining about the crudeness and primitive conditions found at the hotel and the town. Mr. Conrad left and never returned to the area. Back further still, talk rambles on to the time before there was a bridge across the Klamath at Orleans and crossing would depend upon the ferry.

A member of the defunct Klamath River Guides Association and long time friend of Jim Roads and Al Kutzkey, Al Foss is one of the last of the old timers still pulling the sticks on his drift boat and guiding happy clients to the rewards the river might offer. He uses a Lavro fiberglas drift boat and favors Wee Warts with a red butt he draws on them about salmon egg size.

Al sighs as he tells me that the average size of steelhead in the Klamath has decreased and last year his largest was an 8- 1/2 pounder. There have also been fewer studies by D.F.G. in this area of the river than any other. Al hopes all this changes with the selective breeding of steelhead by project F.I.S.H. Al once caught steelhead in the 12 to 15 pound range with regularity near the mouth of Bluff Creek.

At 71, Al is beginning a project and setting his goals and plans around guiding his clients to steelhead he helps to raise. His energy, clean thought and friendly personality make it a joy to be with Al Foss, river guide and conservationist. How can you pass up an opportunity to fish with someone who is part of Klamath River's history.

Jack "The Swede" Husberg

Jack rowed his wooden boat at the mouth of the Klamath River until he was 88 years of age. Simply known as "The Swede" Jack was the first person mentioned by almost everyone I interviewed.His dynamic personality seemed to fit in quite well at the mouth were so many people pursue the act of fishing so very close together. Many of the tourists and famous people to visit Klamath fished with "The Swede" and were rewarded by his skill. Jack was almost always rowing one of the boats closest to the surf, pulling hard on the oars in the flow of an outgoing tide. He was the best of the "white" guides at the mouth and rivaled the Indian guides' success.

Klamath River

Legend

(solid line)	Paved Road
(double dashed line)	Dirt Road
2rm	River Miles
▲	Campground
(shield)	Interstate
(shield)	U.S. Route
(oval)	State Route

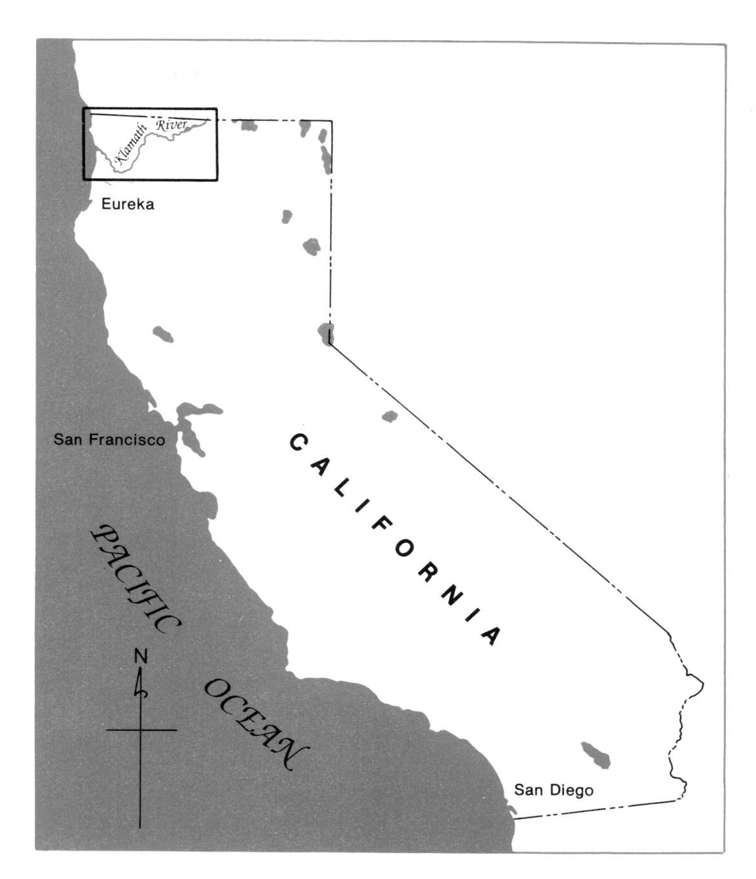

Map 1

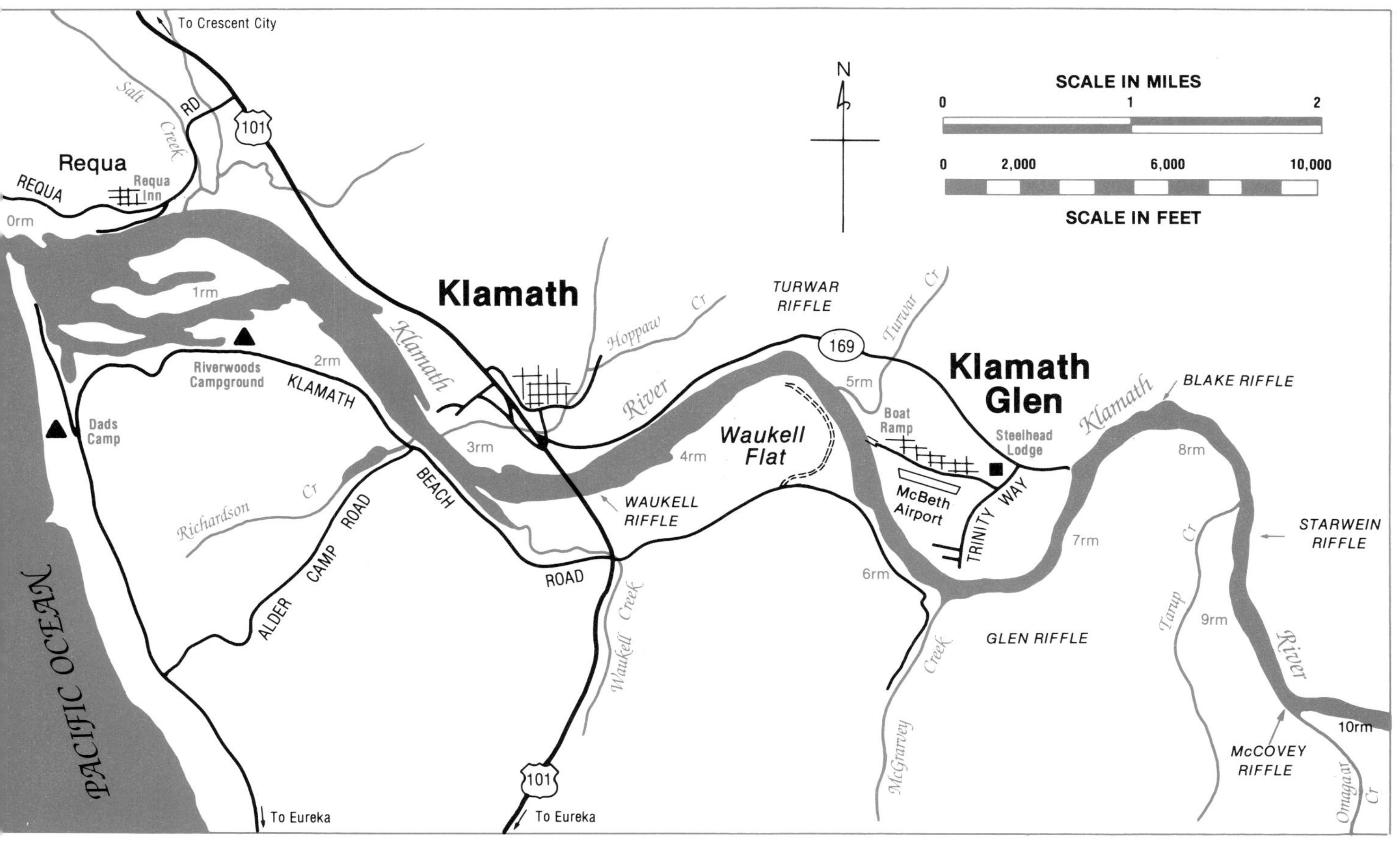

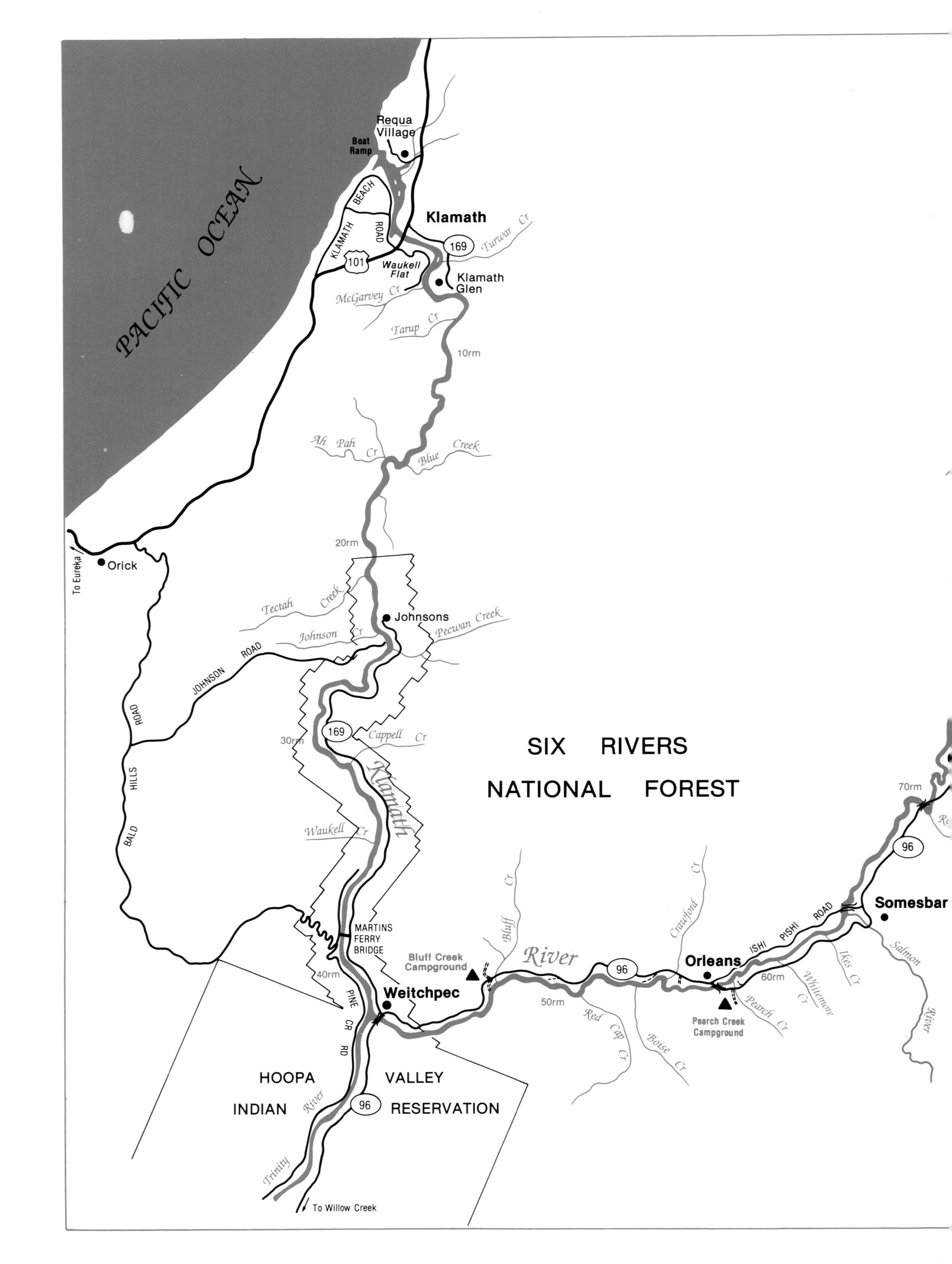

PACIFIC OCEAN
Requa Village
Boat Ramp
KLAMATH BEACH ROAD
Klamath
169
Turwar Cr
101
Waukell Flat
Klamath Glen
McGarvey Cr
Tarup Cr
10rm
Ah Pah Cr
Blue Creek
20rm
To Eureka
Orick
Tectah Creek
Johnsons
Johnson Cr
Pecwan Creek
JOHNSON ROAD
ROAD
169
30rm
Cappell Cr
Klamath
SIX RIVERS
NATIONAL FOREST
BALD HILLS
Waukell Cr
MARTINS FERRY BRIDGE
Bluff Cr
Bluff Creek Campground
River
Crawford Cr
70rm
96
Somesbar
ISHI PISHI ROAD
Orleans
96
40rm
Weitchpec
50rm
Red Cap Cr
Boise Cr
60rm
Pearch Creek Campground
Pearch Cr
Whitemore Cr
Ikes Cr
Salmon River
PINE CR RD
HOOPA VALLEY
INDIAN RESERVATION
River
96
Trinity
To Willow Creek

Klamath River

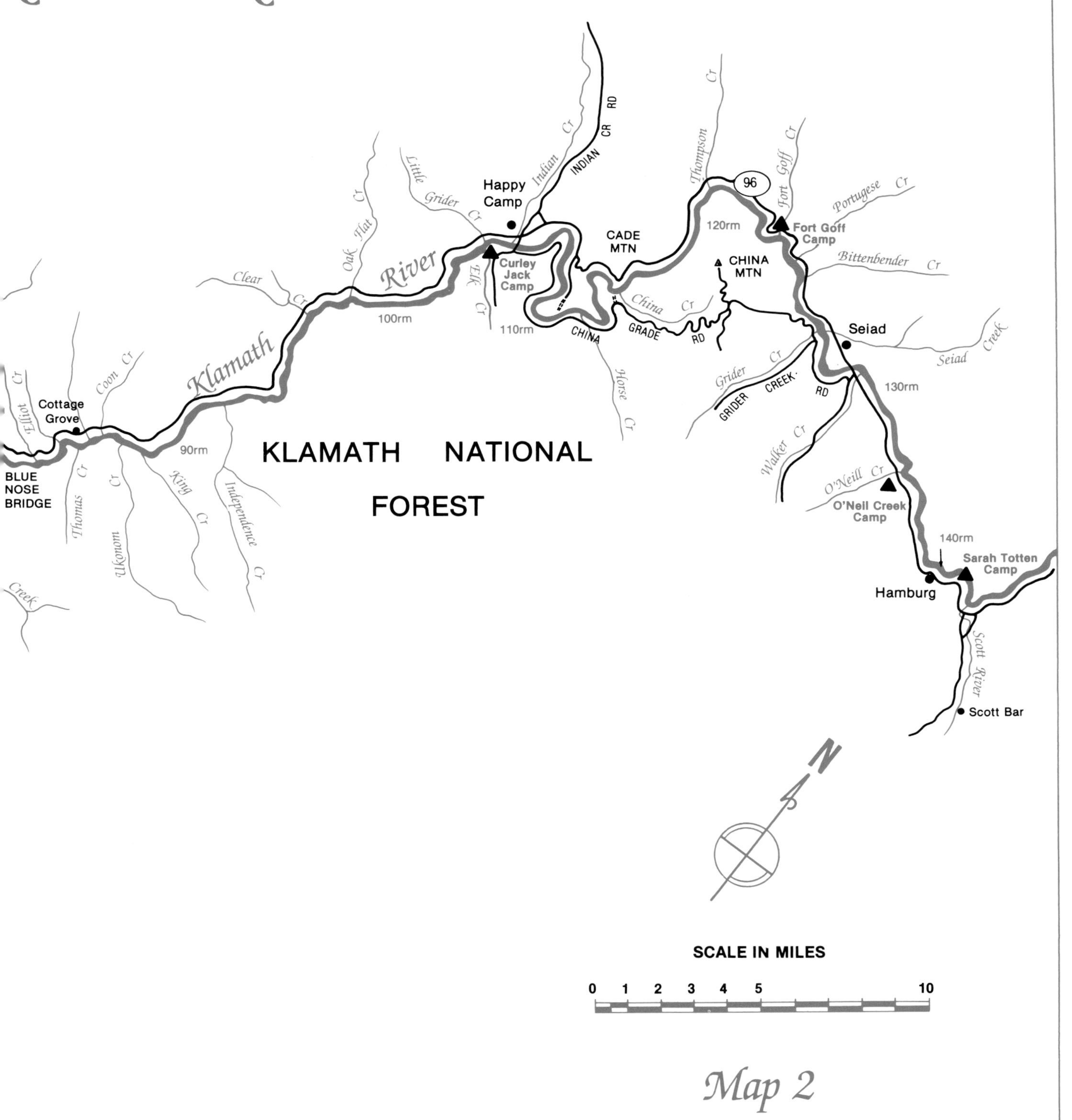

Map 2

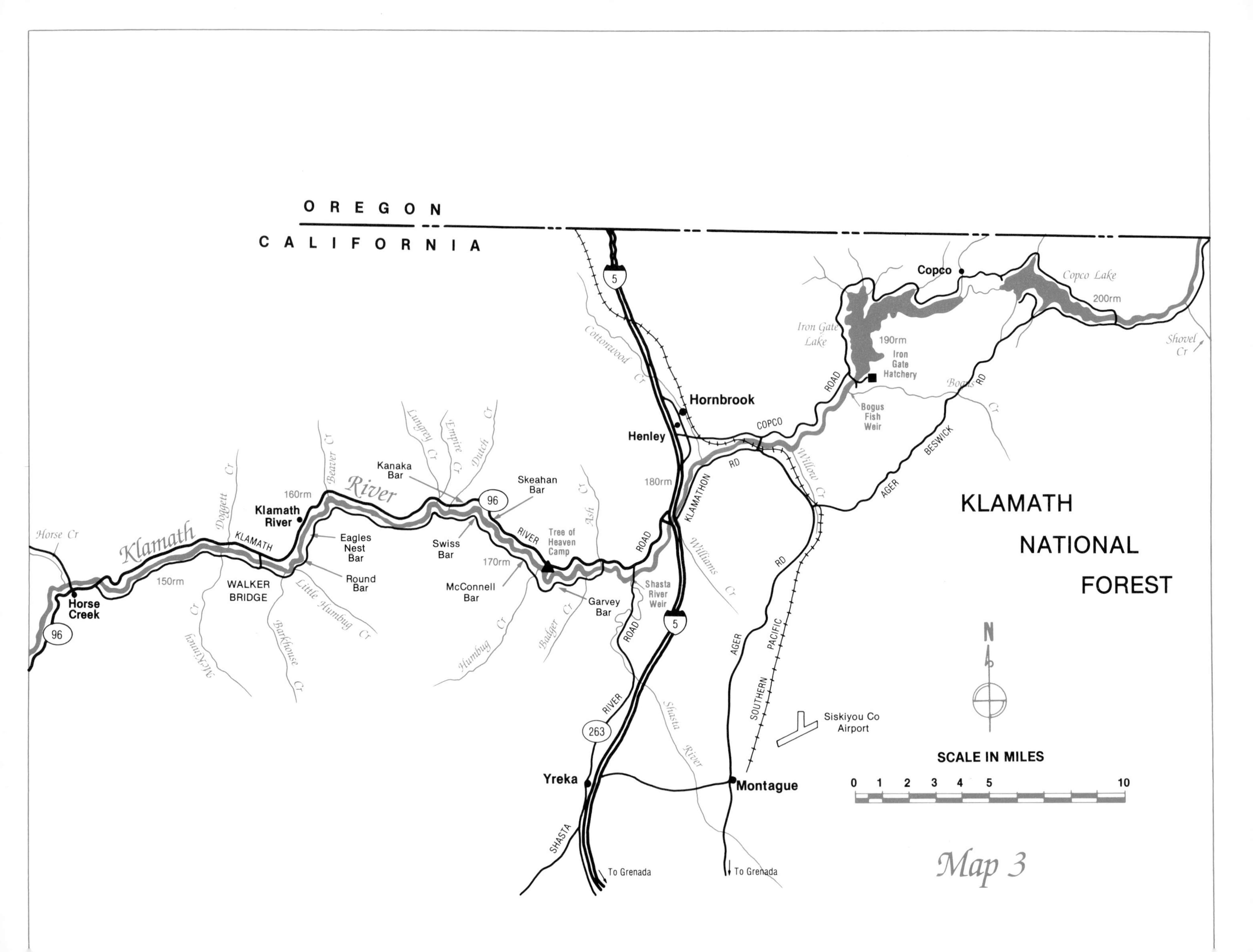
OREGON
CALIFORNIA
KLAMATH NATIONAL FOREST
Copco
Copco Lake
200rm
Shovel Cr
Iron Gate Lake
190rm
Iron Gate Hatchery
Bogus Fish Weir
Bogus Cr
COPCO ROAD
BESWICK AGER RD
Hornbrook
Henley
180rm
Willow Cr
KLAMATHON RD
Cottonwood Cr
Williams Cr
AGER RD
SOUTHERN PACIFIC
Siskiyou Co Airport
Montague
To Grenada
Yreka
SHASTA
263
RIVER ROAD
Shasta River
Shasta River Weir
5
96
Garvey Bar
Ash Cr
Badger Cr
Tree of Heaven Camp
RIVER
170rm
McConnell Bar
Humbug Cr
Skeahan Bar
Swiss Bar
Kanaka Bar
Dutch Cr
Empire Cr
Lungrey Cr
River
Beaver Cr
Eagles Nest Bar
Round Bar
Little Humbug Cr
Barkhouse Cr
160rm
Klamath River
KLAMATH
WALKER BRIDGE
Doggett Cr
McKinney Cr
150rm
Klamath
Horse Creek
Horse Cr
N
SCALE IN MILES
0 1 2 3 4 5 10
Map 3

Zane Grey

Many famous anglers have plied the waters of the Klamath, though few have written of their fishing adventures. This has made the history of fishing and fishing techniques all the harder to research. One of the great writers visited the Klamath several times fishing both alone and with Ed Hughes as his guide. A story appeared in *Outdoor America* in 1923, a publication of the Isaac Walton League of America, by Zane Grey. Zane wrote about a 57-pound salmon he caught at the mouth of the Klamath River using an eight-ounce bass rod.

Grey wrote: "Some miles below Crescent City, we came to a quaint little village called Requa. All we knew of it was that it was the place where we had to ferry across the Klamath River, indeed the whole place smelled fishy."

Not really planning to fish the Klamath on his way between his beloved Rogue and the Eel, Grey saw enough in Klamath to gain his interest when three young men showed him three Chinook salmon averaging 30 pounds and several large steelhead.

Fishing the next day, Grey further relates: "Fish were breaking everywhere. Pelicans were soaring and swooping and smashing the water. Myriads of sea gulls were flying and screaming over the long sand bar. I rowed straight for the mouth of the river to get into the narrow channel, where my advisor earnestly solicited me to go. There was indeed a contest, and the sea was slowly conquering, driving the river back."

It must have been an incoming tide on which Grey was fishing.

Grey goes on: "An irresistibly powerful fish ponderously attached himself to my spoon and made straight for the other skiffs with their network of anchor and hand lines."

Grey went on to explain that few of the fishermen were using rods that day and most were fishing with hand lines. As the fish screamed line from Grey's reel, he wrote: "The whizzing of my reel began to lessen after a time. I calculated that it was because the line had become fouled on some of the anchor ropes. We cleared the first skiff, I had to pass my rod between the second skiff and the anchor rope. It went under water! I got free of the anchor rope as all around Indians and natives were helpful."

It is interesting that Grey obviously refers to the locals as natives and makes a distinction between natives and Indians. Grey goes on to tell how he fought the beast of a salmon on his 8-ounce bass rod.

On boating the fish Grey tells us, "eventually he gave and we lifted him aboard. Broad and long and heavy, silvery and white, with faint spots and specks, and a delicate shimmering lustre, with the great sweep of tail and cruel, wide beaked jaws. We rowed back to the boat dock and weighed the fish at 57 pounds." The fish was no doubt a male.

This story gives us a good idea of what the Klamath was like in earlier times when no doubt the average size of the salmon was larger. Zane Grey fished on the upper and lower Klamath River and found its steelhead almost as willing to take a fly as those of the Rogue.

Klamath River White Water Daredevil Race

One of the most amazing races ever held on the Klamath River was the White Water Daredevil Race. Using small boats powered by low horsepower outboards, daring racers challenged the full 180 mile length of the Klamath River. The race started above highway 99 near Yreka and continued downstream to the mouth of the river. This two day race included all of the rapids in the Klamath River with the exception of Ishi Pishi Falls which was the only portage of the journey. It was a truly incredible feat to accomplish and the race lasted six years during the 1940s. The first winners, Oscar Tayler and Slim Coates, used an Evinrude 4 lite to negotiate the river and won in a time of 2 days, 12 hours, and 18 minutes. Each of the proceeding years the time was bettered and second year winners, Jack McKeller and Ron Gensaw lowered the winning time to 2 days, 11 hours, and 49 minutes. By the final year the time was so fast that everyone lost interest and Alvin Larson won in under 8 hours using a 25 HP motor on his small boat.

It was the nature of the white water in the Klamath River that made this race for daredevils only. They jumped the quick drops and rode out the slots, crashing curls, and at times swamped their boats. One of the most difficult areas was

Jack McKeller and Ron Gensaw arm in arm after winning the Klamath white water race while Eddie Spott looks on. Del Norte Historical Society photo

the Big Ikes below Ishi Pishi Falls. After much studying, it was decided that it could be done. Standing by on the downstream side, Bert Pluvough filmed as Ron Gensaw leaped the curl at the top, flew straight into the air and plowed nose first into the Klamath, swamping but not sinking his boat. A great scream of triumph left Ron's lips. Each boat had less and less trouble as they climbed up and over the curl and leaped down the river. After viewing films of this race, I was surprised that it was completed without fatalities. It was indeed a race for daredevils.

Bert Pluvough and Harold Melvin were responsible for initiating the races and were in all of them. Bert had more second place finishes than anyone, but never managed to win the $600 first prize.

Red Rat's Haven

Located downstream from Bluff Creek was a cabin that gained fame as Red Rat's Haven. It was referred to by many names, including Hilton's Cabin, and was occupied by Henry Hilton, the inventor of one of the Klamath River's most enduring fly patterns, the Silver Hilton. This cabin was known to have provided lodging to many of fly fishing's colorful characters during the 1920s and 1930s. The Silver Hilton pattern was invented here in those early years of steelhead fly fishing.

This midriver area of the Klamath, from the confluence with the Trinity at Weitchpec, upstream to Happy Camp, was where the very best fly fishing for steelhead could be found. Many early flies and fishing ideas for angling with a fly rod were bandied about in the cabin called Red Rat's Haven before being put to the test in the river the following morning.

Bud Johnson

In the early days of fly fishing, Bud Johnson had the opportunity to share riffles and fish with some of the founding fathers of California steelhead fly fishing. Learning from the likes of Jim Pray, Lloyd and Gene Silvius and Walter Thorenson, Bud is one of the long-time fishing faithfuls on the Klamath River.

He developed a green bodied chenille fly for a

warden friend, Jim Bates, and called the fly the Warden Special after his friend. He is also the only person to have caught and documented an Atlantic salmon from the Klamath River. Before you throw up your hands in disbelief, let me assure you that the California Department of Fish and Game tried to import Atlantic salmon to the Klamath River in the 1940s. It was a failed attempt and when Bud caught his fish, he wasn't certain exactly what he had. He took the fish to Vern's Tackle, and Vern Flachsman took the fish to the Department of Fish and Game where a biologist told them it was indeed an Atlantic salmon.

Today, Bud stays at the Redwood Rest Resort and either fly fishes or casts spinners in Blake's Riffle or Starwein Riffle, his two favorites.

Bluff Creek Resort

Gephart's was the oldest private campground in the Bluff Creek area and preceded Bluff Creek Resort. Originally the Adornele Ranch, it was made into a cafe by Jack Rollen. Bluff Creek Resort is now owned by Lon and Chris Saunders. It still is a favorite R.V. park and campground for steelheaders. The Fred Bear Lodge, which was another in this area, was washed out in the 1964 flood.

Nice sturgeon caught near Bluff Creek. Kutzkey Lodge photo

Orleans Hotel

Midriver fly fishing has long been famous at the town of Orleans on the Klamath River and the Orleans Hotel has been the meeting and congregating spot for fishermen and women for over 70 years. It was built by the Van Pelts in the early 1900s, and has survived two major floods (although there was water in the hotel during both). The Orleans Hotel remains rustic and original.

Several guides worked out of the hotel, and longtime guide Al Foss was one of several owners. The hotel itself remains essentially the same as it was in the early years, and some of its more fastidious visitors have found it to be lacking in the more modern conveniences.

Francis Head

Francis Head, from Happy Camp on the Klamath River, tied many of the flies used by area fly casters and guides alike. Her delicate touch tied many of the exacting patterns of the Klamath River, and she was responsible for many happy hours enjoyed in the early pursuit of steelhead. She was particularly fond of the upright, single wing, style. Francis also guided many fly fishers for steelhead on the Klamath River near Happy Camp.

Peter Schwab

It was very frustrating for me to go to Yreka, where Peter Schwab lived, and find no one who remembered him and nothing at all about him in the Siskiyou Historical Society. The fact that he was important to fly fishing on the Klamath I learned only from Trey Combs' book *Steelhead Fly Fishing and Flies*, and it seemed that if Mr. Schwab had not written letters and corresponded with Ralph Wahl (of Washington) he might well have been lost to Klamath River angling history.

Peter Schwab was a pioneer in the upper Klamath River's fly fishing development and is credited with such flies as the Brass Hat, Queen Bess and Bobby Dunn. An Easterner transplanted to the Klamath River near Hornbrook, Schwab's home was named the Swallows, and a roadhouse along highway 96 still bears that name. (I could not find out if it was indeed the same building; no one knew of him there.)

Schwab was highly prejudiced towards Klamath River steelhead and once wrote that there were "more steelhead in the Klamath River than in the entire state of Oregon." He and his wife Bess, for whom the Queen Bess fly was named, fished the Klamath River in the 1940s, and on October 22, 1945, Bess caught a 10-pound Klamath River steelhead with the fly that bears her name.

His research and experiments with silk fly lines showed promise, but were ill timed and became outdated by other superior synthetic lines before they were perfected. Peter Schwab died in 1955 in Florida. He never got around to writing the book he planned about detailing his secrets and innovations in fly lines.

Joe B. Clyburn

Born in Grants Pass, Oregon in the year 1911, Joe and his family moved to Lime Gulch on the Klamath River in 1916 and bought 160 acres for $500. As a school boy Joe walked a three mile trail each morning on his way to the Honolulu Schoolhouse and returned home from a daily six mile walk. Later, from 1917 to 1918, the state used prisoners from San Quentin to make a road along that trail. Joe's family crossed the Klamath in a cable cart that sometimes carried the entire family in one trip. Early times for Klamath River families were hard and these days, at 78, Joe can still walk many a younger person into the ground.

Like many raised during these times, Joe worked the mines and timber from his youth until he retired. In the 1930s, Joe worked for the United States Forest Service putting in many of the roads that crisscross Siskiyou County. He also had one brief experience at mining, but found it much too dangerous for his liking. Searching for gold by hand drilling and setting charges were not Joe's cup of tea. The fresh air of the outdoors went along with logging and Joe worked 29 years for the Fruit Growers Supply harvesting trees that would be turned into pallets, bins and boxes for the fruit industry in the Sacramento and San Jaquin valleys of central California.

Joe was a hardy lumberjack who with only a cross cut saw, axe and a spring board or two would bring down the mighty trees that bordered every stream in Klamath Country. Chopping an undercut with an axe, raising himself as much as 4 to 5 feet on a spring board and using a hand saw to fall cedar and sugar pine as large as 10 or 15 feet in diameter were done in a day's work. With the coming of the chainsaw, methods in logging changed and a new era in logging began.

Today at 78, Joe has become a wildlife photographer of local renown. His photos are of genuinely rare objects and require patience found in

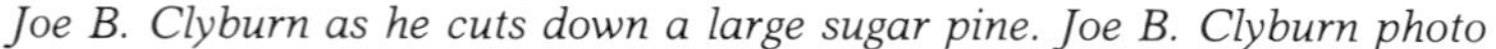

Joe B. Clyburn as he cuts down a large sugar pine. Joe B. Clyburn photo

few people in these fast paced days. The wildlife photos in this book are only a small sample of Joe's work and he presents slide shows for groups in the Yreka area. Taking the photos, Joe gets not only the walking and the exercise he needs but many long hours of tense hiding. The time it takes to locate your subject and then find a vantage point that provides an unobstructed shot are hard enough let alone the long hours spent waiting, sometimes in vain or for just one chance at a photo.

This seldom seen Bobcat seems to be posing for the camera. Joe B. Clyburn photo

Once in the chill of winter Joe spent the morning tracking four large blacktail bucks and another four hours lying still as the snow began to fall. Just as the bucks lined up and moved into the open for a clear shot, Joe realized the shutter had frozen on his camera and a long day went for nothing.

Joe's also a steelheader of some skill and spends many days tossing lures for Klamath River iron heads. Joe acknowledges fishing is a lot tougher these days and 1987 was a very slow year for him. Using mostly Rooster Tails, Joe has caught many steelhead from the Klamath both on lure and fly. His largest steelhead was a 13-pound hen caught downriver near the mouth of the Salmon River.

Joe B. Clyburn is an original pioneer on the Klamath River.

Marsaw's Fish Smoking

Beverly and Leon "Frenchy" Marsaw ran their smokehouse on Arrow Mills Road in Terwer Valley until 1978 and smoked many of the fish caught by sport fishermen. Every year from May until October, there would be a column of smoke rising from the smokehouse and the grand smell of sweet wood smoke in the air. Having a place to get your fish smoked was a definite advantage for many of the tourists that frequented Klamath in its peak years of fishing in the 1950s and 1960s. During its fifth year of smoking fish, the Marsaw's also began a canning facility where smokehouse customers could do their own canning.

In one year, 1954, 2800 pounds of steelhead was smoked in the entire state of California, and 1600 pounds of that was smoked at the Marsaw Smoker. (D.F.G. required the filing of forms reporting the amounts of fish smoked at all commercial smoke houses.) Salmon composed the bulk of the weight and one-half ton was smoked every day. This seems incredible but they were also smoking ocean caught fish.

The biggest steelhead that was smoked by the Marsaw's was a 26-pounder caught in the Klamath River in August, 1954. The largest salmon was an ugly 46-pound male. There was also an 11-foot sturgeon that was cleaned for a 5.00 fee. So many sturgeon began to come in that Bev upped the price to 10.00 and finally left a note saying "clean your own damn sturgeon." Many tourists remember the Marsaw Smokehouse and the tasty fish they had cured there.

Fred Ruff

In the middle of Scott Valley, while fishing the Scott River, I met one of the finest fishermen I have ever known. Fred Ruff resides in Fort Jones and may have no equal in his fishing success on the Scott River. His techniques have proven valid on many of the rivers I have fished and I'll always know I'm a better angler for having known Fred.

Fred uses a unique approach when drifting the Scott River. The Scott is a small stream, usually 60 to 90 feet wide. A rod, with a plug attached, is set in its holder and fished dead center of the boat. On both sides the individuals in the front seats cast and roll Glo Bugs or plastic attractors. (Fred does not allow bait in his boat!) Most steelhead are caught on the Glo Bugs and Fred thinks the plug helps move the fish to the side so they're in the proper position for the cast. When snagged, Fred often lays down the rod that is hung up and fishes with his backup rod. Many times the snagged rod works itself free by the time Fred returns to it. Fred taught me the virtue of patience and planning when confronted with a problem.

Klamath River Guide Association

One of the first collective associations of guides in California was formed on the Klamath River in 1960. The very independent nature of guides, who are in fact individual contractors and who each have their own ideas of how to run a business, makes any collective movement a difficult effort. It lasted for a period of six years and helped to better relations between the guides and the CDFG which helped to organize the association.

The Charter Members were: Jim Roads Bill McCorkle Al Kutzkey Ed Morris Roy Barnes Ed

Burton Jim Proctor Tom Crocker John Rider Mike Allen Ron Throgmorton Andy Stone Jeff Throgmorton Tim Kutzkey Hal Borg Dave Roads Al Foss Bob DeNardi

The work of Jim Roads, Jim Proctor and Bill Claypole helped to keep the group meeting and discussing river problems. And the group enhanced some streams by clearing them from obstructions.

Eventually interest in the organization ebbed. Al Kutzkey was elected president and then left the group, never to attend another meeting. The association worked toward getting a water release agreement from the Trinity River and Lewiston Dam as well as minimum release agreements for the Klamath from Iron Gate Dam – so all was not lost.

Today, there are three guide associations in California, all dealing with the problems that face our fisheries and wildlife in our local areas. Guides feel they are some of the best information sources the Department of Fish and Game has because of the large number of days and hours that they spend on the river. It is a definite struggle to achieve a collective decision and a course of action among such strong willed individuals. However, it is a fact that by organizing together and voicing collective concerns guides can gain more influence in forming laws and future developments that may threaten our fisheries.

Captain Don Chapman

Among those whose lives have been of great help to the Klamath River was Captain Don Chapman, Fish and Game Warden for Siskiyou County for 25 years. He rode the hills astride a big white mare and developed a reputation for being in two places at once. He was a hard man who policed the river during the 1930s, '40s and early '50s when it was common practice for locals to spear salmon in the smaller streams throughout the county. Up until about 1930 spearing fish was not illegal.

Joe Clyburn, who was born in 1911, remembers as a boy going to town and buying toggle spears to kill salmon. "A regular spear would pull right back out," explained Joe, "and you had to push the fish in front of you until you got it out of the water. Toggle spears changed all that because they bent over from hinged (toggled) points that held onto the fish and rarely pulled out."

When I worked for CDFG in the area of the Shasta River fish weir, there were several people told me stories about how Captain Chapman who had caught them stealing fish from the fish trap at the weir or snagging. They all remembered him as a mean son-of-a-gun, but I suppose it's really a matter of perspective. Few persons speak kindly of their adversary let alone those who have arrested them.

Riding that big white mare dressed in the old style uniform with a wide brim mountie hat, Captain Don Chapman will always be a legend on the Klamath River.

Myers Brothers

Elmer, Chico and E. Larry Myers came to the Klamath from Oakland and purchased the old Cates Fishing Resort. Their family has remained in Klamath for over 40 years. There was reference to Elmer in the Mel Marshall book titled *Steelhead* for his excellence as a spinner fisherman. The two shared an autumn day fishing spinners on Blue Creek Riffle with Harry Hammond, another Klamath hardware fisherman. Both Elmer and Harry repeatedly caught steelhead, while the novice skills of Mr. Marshall left him without eliciting a strike. Fishing the exact same tackle, it became obvious that the only difference was in presentation of the lures. Elmer was the fisherman of the Myers clan and fished as often as he could on the Klamath. Most years he landed well over 200 steelhead, not counting half-pounders, but it was another brother, Roy Myers who caught a 25-pound steelhead while visiting his three brothers in Klamath. This must have been a galling experience for Elmer who spent nearly every day of the year casting spinners from the bank somewhere on the Klamath River.

Harold Delponte

Born in Klamath Country in 1916, Harold DelPonte has lived his entire life in the town of Klamath. Though he has never once put a line in the river, Harold has been the official weatherman in Klamath these past 42 years beginning in 1947. While growing up on his father's dairy in

Terwer Valley, he fished in Terwer Creek as a boy. He says: "There was a spring steelhead run in that creek you wouldn't believe."

One day, following some of the men working in the area, the young DelPonte and his schoolmate John McMillian watched as steelhead after steelhead were snagged from beneath root wads, jerked to the surface and shot with a .22 rifle. One hundred and twenty-seven steelhead were killed in all!

Another story he told me occured when he and the young McMillan took their dogs to the creek to play fetch. There were so many steelhead making wakes in the shallow riffles in Terwer Creek that whenever they saw fish they would toss a rock in that direction and their dogs would proceed to retrieve a steelhead.

From his weather statistics the climate of the lower Klamath River can be easily understood. The warmest month of the year, August, averages 59.3 degrees and the coldest month, January, averages 49.9 degrees. "Around here you can just keep your flannel shirt on year round," says Harold. In 41 years there has been a total of 14 days in which it rained over 5 inches per day and there were 35 months where the total rainfall exceed 20 inches per month. In 41 years it has never reached 100 degrees in Klamath. On June 4, 1960, the temperature peaked with the record of 98 degrees. There have only been 17 days that were over 90 degrees. It is a wet climate and there have been eight years with over 100 inches of rainfall. They were: 1956-1957, 1957-1958, 1970-1971, 1972-1973, 1973-1974, 1981-1982, 1982-1983, 1983-1984. The wettest month was November 1973 when 35.3 inches of precipitation fell in Klamath. "It rained every day of the month except the 19th and over an inch every day it rained," recalls Mr. DelPonte, former Del Norte county Supervisor and Mr. Weatherman on the river for 41 years.

Harold told me a story about Jack Morris, former owner of Blue Creek Lodge. It seems that whenever Jack was heading upriver and ran across an old Indian named Seely Griffin, he would ask Seely to predict the weather and like a wise Indian sage, Griffin always seemed to predict the weather correctly. One day Jack asked Seely how he could forecst the weather with such accuracy, to which Seely replied: "I listen to the radio."

Klamath Camper Corral was started by Harold DelPonte in 1972 and was sold six years later. Today he is the owner and proprietor of Klamath's Tour through Tree which he started in 1976. It is with pride that Harold states: "I haven't once raised my prices, it's still one dollar." The hole in the tree was cut by his nephew, Darol Damm, and is large enough for most vehicles to drive through. Darol Damm and his wife, Linda, now are owners of the Damm Drifter Tackle Shop in Klamath Glen and Darol is one of the leading fishing guides in the state.

Klamath Queen

Alvin Larson, the son of Elsie and Baldy Larson, was one of the boating giants on the Klamath River. Klamath Queen Jet Boat Tours operated by Requa Docks from 1965 through 1984, was the longest running jet boat service on the river. The *Klamath Queen* was 46 feet in length with a 14 foot beam and was capable of hauling 60 passengers. The jet boat trips covered 64 miles of river and had a midday break for lunch at the Larson Lodge built upriver near Ryersons Rock.

Jim Barneburg was one of the regular drivers of the "Queen" and ran the boat for many years. Other operators included Court Boice of Boice Boats, who built many of Alvin Larson's boats, including the *Klamath Queen*. The last tour driver was Alvin's son, John Larson.

There are many people whose only view of the Klamath River came from the trip they took on the *Queen*. It will long be remembered as *the* jet boat tour on the Klamath River.

With the death of Alvin Larson, the Larson family has sold Requa Docks and ceased the jet boat tours that helped make the Klamath River famous. After a three year absence, new owners have another new boat, the *Requa Queen*, and it is again taking passengers upriver.

Bob Steele

Bob Steele was one of the early jet boat guides on the lower Klamath River and started Steelhead Lodge in Klamath Glen. (Steelhead Lodge is perhaps the most popular place to eat dinner in Klamath.)

Klamath Queen in June 1982. Mary Larson photo

After some years off the river, Bob Steele returned for the 1988 season. His new business cards state his claim to fame as "the guide who guided Curt Gowdy." Of course I'll always remember Curt Gowdy on an outdoor TV show in the mid 1970s when talking about the total decline and demise of the great Klamath River steelhead.

Somes Bar Lodge

Jeff and Ron Throgmorton were both charter members of the Klamath River Guides Association and today their younger brother, Brad, runs Somes Bar Lodge near the town of the same name. Though not one of the early lodges, Somes Bar Lodge deserves mention because of the Throgmorton's contributions to Klamath River angling.

Somes Bar Lodge is near the mouth of the Salmon River and in recent times much of the lodges business has been rafting on both the Klamath and Salmon rivers. The Cal/Salmon, as it's recently been called because of the more famous Salmon River in Idaho, has some great early spring rafting with several class IV and class V rapids. Each summer the staff at the lodge makes an exodus and floats downriver on the Klamath to the Pacific Ocean some 50 miles away.

Though the largest steelhead taken at the lodge came from the Salmon, a 14-pound buck, there was a 12 1/2 pound female, 34 1/2 inches long and very thin caught on the Klamath in 1987. I heard while at the lodge about angler Charlie Shap who was said to have caught a 25-pound steelhead in the Salmon River just below the forks of the Salmon.

Lloyd Silvius

Lloyd Silvius, baker and master fly tier, made many contributions to early fly fishing on the Eel and Klamath rivers. The Nite Owl and Brindle Bug are two flies originally tied and credited to Mr. Silvius. He tied flies for Blue Creek Lodge in the 1940s and 1950s and he later opened a fly shop in Eureka, California. For his many years of fly tying and other contributions to steelhead fly fishing, Lloyd Silvius will always be recognized as an important figure on the Klamath River. Silvius and his beautiful flies are remembered by Mabel Morris: "Lloyd treated each and every fly like it was a delicate living creature." We remember you Mr. Silvius!

Safford's Island

Sitting in the river about one and a half miles from the mouth of the Klamath River was a large island. It was there many years with its rich soil. Safford's Island had flowers, shrubs and trees, although there weren't any conifers found on the island. Trilliums, violets, foxglove, mullein, daisies, buttercups, dandelions and many other flowers grew well. Indian currant, gooseberry, blackberry, hazelnut, thimbleberry, elderberry and salmonberry made the island a delicious gathering spot for local people. Deer, raccoons, skunks and mink also made the island their home.

There was a house in the center of the island

Dedication of the Douglas Memorial Bridge in 1926. Del Norte Historical Society photo

that had an orchard with apple and plum trees. It was occupied by John Safford, a soldier who came to Klamath in the early 1890s.

A Fishermen's Carnival was held on the island before the Klamath River was closed to commercial fishing. The locals would all be in attendance and games such as tug-of-war, foot races and wrestling were played. A certain stick game was rough and tough and usually pitted a white team against an Indian team. The Fishermen's Cannery was built near the southern tip of the island and a number of cabins were built there for the fishermen.

When excavations were made for piers for the Douglas Memorial Bridge in the late 1920s, sand and gravel were dumped in the channel below the bridge. The gravel washed downstream and filled the channel at the head of the Norris Riffle, long since gone. This moved the current over to the north shore and when the 1955 flood rose to its peak, the main current met Stafford's Island head on. When the flood waters receded, three fourths of the island had been washed away. The 1964 flood finished the job and Stafford's Island is no more. Fond memories of this 83-acre island still remain in the minds of many of the people raised in Klamath.

Jim Gensaw

Yurok Indian and elder of the Gensaw family, Jim Gensaw lived nearly his whole life, which is believed to have spanned 108 years, on the Klamath. He was born at Marrep on the Klamath River in 1845. His age was calculated on the basis of his memories of the 1861-1862 flood when he was 16 or 17 years old.

Jimmy did a lot of fishing, hunted with bow and arrow and was an expert at snaring deer. About 1869, he came to Requa and worked with Captain Spott hauling freight to the gold mines at Gold Bluffs, using dugout boats that the Indians built by burning out giant redwood logs. Jimmy died in 1953 at his foster daughter's (Florence Shaughnessy) home in Requa.

Captain Crone

In the summer of 1902, a curious craft entered the Klamath River. Locals soon learned that it was a gold mining dredge brought from the Sacramento River and was proposed to be taken upriver to the mines. On board was a salty dog of a captain and a crew that included a young Dane, William Crone, who was never to leave this area. The dredger never reached the gold fields, the captain died of a heart attack, and the young boy of 19 remained in this new land he dearly loved.

During the summer months Requa was a bustling place with people coming from afar to work in the canneries. Young Crone also worked for the cannery and tried his luck fishing for salmon with a gill net.

Work was often scarce and Crone got a job as a sailor aboard the *Dawn*, which replaced the *Lady Mine* on route from the Klamath. It was on this boat that he became a regular member of the crew. In the summer of 1908, the schooner *Dawn* struck a submerged rock near Trinidad and was wrecked.

Crone received financial backing and bought his own boat, the *Coaster*, a rugged twin screw ship that was ideally suited for coastal trade. It was aboard the *Coaster* that he received the title he was to bear for the rest of his life. "Captain of the *Coaster*." He was a skilled and competent sailor but like many sailors Captain Crone was very superstitious and would never sail on Friday which was his personal bad luck day.

The exploits of the Captain were many, but as age mellowed him, he purchased the Requa Inn and ran it for some years. He was public spirited and when the influenza epidemic struck the area, he did his best administering to the needy from his faithful whiskey bottle.

Some Other Camps

There were many resorts along the lower river that were important to the growing popularity of the Klamath. During the 1920s and through the 1950s, fishing was at its peak and the river's reputation as the salmon and steelhead capitol of California was built.

Klamath Glen Resort

Situated on the banks of the Klamath, this resort was first washed away in 1927 and has been underwater many times since. It's a favorite with those who like to gaze at the river from their campsite. Early visitors to the Klamath Glen Resort included Dick Powell and June Allison.

Today it is a resort n wheels and the office, washrooms, etc., are built on trailers so they can be towed to high ground before the rainy season.

Sportsmen

Frank Bosch, the last stagecoach driver and ferryman on the Klamath, started his camp on the south bank of the river. Today it is a membership campground open only to individuals who buy into the group of campgrounds offered by the company. Security guards and gates keep it very private.

Shorty's Camp

Shorty Conners was one of the colorful figures of the town of Klamath and his camp was one of the earliest fishing camps on the river. Starting in the days of the Model T, the camp flourished in the 1920s and had many boats tied to its docks. Shorty was one of the real old timers of Klamath and loved to fish the mouth of the river. Shorty's Camp had docks with 150 rental boats for guest fishing the mouth of the river.

Shorty's Camp – run by the notorious Shorty Conners. Mable Morris photo

Klamath Cove

This resort was built by Harrison Williams and has survived in spite of time, floods and ownership changes. It is located at the mouth of the river on the south bank. The present owners know little of its history, but it was one of the early camps. At one time it was owned by the Morris family of Blue Creek Lodge.

Roy Rook's Terwer Resort

Klamath Glen's present boat ramp was named for Roy Rook, one of the resilient resort owners who fought back from the floods in 1955 and 1964. After the 1955 flood, Roy looked at his flood damaged resort and flatly stated: "I'll be back in business by summer. It's not that bad." It is located right next to the boat ramp and is one of the many R.V. parks in Klamath.

Redwood Rest

Redwood Rest was built by one of Klamath's first families, Charles and Emma McBeth, who operated it for many years. Cabins built beneath one of the last stands of native growth redwood separate Redwood Rest from other resorts in the area. The cabins have Indian names and a huge wooden Indian was carved and stands at the entrance. It is still one of the most attractive campgrounds and resorts. Many guides stay there.

Fortain's Camp

This camp is important because it was the location of Klamath's first airport. Today's airport is about three miles further inland and has less fog to obscure and complicate air traffic. Today the former location of Fortain's Camp is occupied by Riverwoods Campground owned by Chub and Judy Morris.

Paul's Cannery

Beginning in 1933, Paul's Cannery served sport fishermen and is one of the remaining area landmarks. Today it is a bar and grill that's also famous for its salmon jerky.

Crivellis

Built and then rebuilt after the floods, Crivellis has been one of the areas best restaurants for over 40 years. At one time the bar was adorned with the fishing rods of many famous anglers who visited the Klamath such as Bing Crosby, Zane Grey and Dick Powell.

One night at a gathering in Crivellis, rod builder Walton Powell, of Powell Rods, entered the bar and began bragging about the strength and flexibility of his rods. He then went out to his car, produced a rod and proclaimed that he could touch the butt and tip together. As he bent the rod into a circle, the fractures popped into breaks and the rod was soon in four distinct and different pieces. Walt, being a proud as well as a stubborn man, ran out to his car and came back into the bar carrying every rod he had brought with him (Walt carried several). He then proceeded to bend each and every rod into a circle and hold it there while smiling defiantly, showing everyone in the bar that he was right. Crivellis is still serving good food. It has been some years since the founder, Babe Crivellis, owned it.

Herd of Roosevelt elk in the Somes Bar area. Joe B. Clyburn photo

5 The Fishing

Throughout the history of the Klamath River, isolation between the upper and lower portions of the river has kept the remote nature of the river intact. There was never a highway or railroad that traveled the entire distance of the Klamath River. The lower 20 miles has remained accessible only by river traffic that in recent years has been restricted to jet boats – necessary for crossing the shallow bars near many of the riffles.

Since the late 1800s, people have attempted to connect the upper and lower river without any success. Since the very first trail was made, Kelsey's, there have been only futile attempts at uniting the river by land. An early account describes the conditions found on the Kelsey Trail: "...travels over this narrow, steep and winding thread along mountain sides, over divides, into deep canyons, balancing on mountain ridges where there is hardly room enough for a horse to step, with each side pitching away into dark bottoms thousands of feet below."

The rugged nature of the terrain has forever kept the Klamath in distinct, separate and remote parts.

Where To Fish

The Klamath is really several different areas, each remote and isolated from the other. This offers anglers unique experiences in several types of settings and climates. The Klamath River is full of change as it flows from Iron Gate Dam to the Pacific Ocean.

There are four major angling areas found along the river:

1. The upper Klamath River, from Iron Gate past Hornbrook and downriver to the mouth of the Scott River. This area also includes the Shasta River and such lodges as Kutzkey's and Beaver Creek.

2. The middle river, from Siead Valley downstream to Weitchpec. This area has much interesting history and is the best fly fishing portion of the river. Jim Roads, Thompson Creek Lodge, Somes Bar Lodge, Al Foss and the historic Orleans Hotel hail or are situated along this section of river.

3. The Trinity River, which has recently been an excellent fishery. Trinity River salmon populations exceed the entire remaining portions of the Klamath River basin. Steelhead are also the largest in the Klamath River Drainage often eight to fourteen pounds!

4. The lower Klamath River, which includes the mouth, Requa, Klamath, Blue Creek, Johnsons, Martins Ferry and so many of the guides and lodges important to the history of fishing on the Klamath River. This is my own choice because it offers a chance at all of the fish before they disperse among the tributaries beginning with the Trinity. Redwood trees, the moderate climate and having first chance at the fish all add up to the reasons I've fished the lower Klamath River each year since 1981.

I remember the first time I saw the lower Klamath. The mouth was alive with activity and even its normally dynamic nature was heightened to a level I've not seen since. It was one of those strange phenomenons which found the anchovies running inside the mouth of the river and dying in the fresh water. Anchovies were everywhere along the edges of the beach, and huge flocks of seagulls fought for the parched and dried carcasses of the dead fish. Formations of brown pelicans swooped across the spit and dove one by one into the estuary making large splashes as they gorged on the abundance of nature.

The beach was crowded with shore casters tossing gobs of lead with spinners attached into the midst of a hundred or more boats. People were picking up the dead anchovies and using them for bait. Here and there someone always seemed to be reeling in a salmon. They were horsed in on heavy gear and a tight line giving no quarter to the prey. Seals were diving and appearing as well as sea lions which rolled their mammoth bodies in grand arches as they chased the salmon and steelhead entering the river. Up the beach there were Native American netters wrestling fish from their nets as well as the coarse shouting that came from one of the Indians who had discovered that one of the seals had beat him to the fish in his net.

On the ocean side people were surf fishing for red-tail perch. Many of those fishing had picked up anchovies to use for bait and were hooking salmon. Fish and Game wardens were running up and down the beach helping people release their fish and the salmon were taking a terrible beating in the surf. They were also advising people not to use a whole anchovy in order to avoid hooking a salmon. It was a sight I'll never forget. The mouth will always be a dynamic location – where the river meets the sea.

There are two major highways that cross the Klamath River, Highway 101 near the coast and Interstate 5 about 175 miles upstream. Both of these provide access to different areas of the river and before you plan a trip to the Klamath River be sure to check maps to determine the best route. If your destination is anywhere other than the lower river, near the town of Klamath, you should come by way of Interstate 5. Highway 96 follows the river downstream all the way to Weitchpec. If you are traveling to the Trinity there are several highways leading to Highway 299 which follows the Trinity River.

Fishing at the mouth of the Klamath River has always been crowded. This photo shows two anchor lines as well as a crowd of shore casters fishing the spit. Del Norte Historical Society photo

About Guides

Depending on where you decide to fish there are many quality lodges and guides on the Klamath River. There are also many others whose reputation is less than credible. Before you hire a guide, try to obtain specific hours you will be fishing, whether other anglers might be added to your party (or did you book the boat) and exactly what kind of fishing you will be doing. These are need to know items that will keep you from booking a disappointing trip. Remember, the best guides book early for a reason, so call ahead to ensure your choice among guides instead of arriving at the river and taking your chances on whoever is left.

Meet The River

Winter steelheading is a rough, tough sport that offers no sympathy to the unprepared. Much of the season is spent fighting the wind and weather or dealing with unfavorable water conditions. There are potentially plenty of problems to dampen one's enthusiasm and all too few minutes spent actually fighting the fish. To really love the sport you must enjoy the fishing and most of the other challenges. Oneness with the river must be felt...as countless casts are made while awaiting a single trembling of the rod tip...the gentle stopping of the drift...and the bite of a fish.

It seems only logical to plan your attack against winter's best storms by knowing the river you fish. Anglers must have a close feeling for each of the many rivers they fish. Coming to understand a river and how to fish it at every water level will add to your productivity and keep those days when you are skunked to a minimum.

Many who fish regularly are completely lost in the rise of the river following a winter storm and spend long periods without being able to fish. During these high, muddy flows fish travel tight to the bank and do not fight the heavy currents that are carrying sand, silt and even gravel. When the water and weather conditions change, it is up to the angler to adjust to nature.

One day, there in the river while feeling its flow, you will come to understand. Watching the disturbance across the gravel bottom the cold won't seem to matter and your thoughts will make you wonder if you've gone nuts – because you won't even care if the fishing is lousy, as long as you are fishing! This is the day you have waited for because by meeting and understanding the river, you have answered the call and become a real steelheader.

Weight Systems

One of the easiest methods of rigging the weight for the terminal tackle is the Klamath cinch, which consists of a piece of surgical tubing attached to a swivel into which a piece of pencil lead is inserted. There are many references to the Klamath Cinch in angling literature including the book *Steelhead* by Mel Marshall. Mr. Marshall refers extensively to the Klamath Cinch in his book copyrighted in 1973 by Winchester Press. He states: "The formal name of this fisherman's friend is the Klamath Cinch. Tied between line and leader, the tubing of the cinch accepts the tip of a pencil sinker, and makes a rig that is virtually snag proof." That's the method for using the Klamath Cinch when drift fishing. He also mentions the usefulness of the Klamath cinch when fishing with lures: "Practically all the wobbling lures like spinners will need extra weight to carry and keep them deep. Use the Klamath Cinch for this."

He goes on to explain how the rigging of the Klamath Cinch does not change the way lighter weighted spinners work. The other advantage he points out is that you will loose fewer lures by using the pencil lead and tubing. Credit for this innovation that has helped anglers in their pursuit of steelhead goes to Vern Flachsman of Vern's Tackle, Klamath California. Though Vern was not a fisherman he was always coming up with gadgets that helped area fishermen. (See Vern Falchsman, Chapter 4.)

The Klamath cinch can be used as a fixed weight when using a three way swivel by tying the line and leader to each remaining end of the swivel. When using a barrel or snap swivel, the Klamath cinch can be used as a sliding sinker. Under usual fishing circumstances you use a sliding weight in slow runs and pools in order to increase your reaction time by allowing the line to slide through the weight – hoping the fish will hold on to the bait a bit longer. In fast water, the fish tend to grab a bait more firmly and often hook themselves.

Surgical tubing and lead come in two sizes, 3/16 inch and 1/4 inch, and the choice is a matter of personal preference. I prefer the larger diameter lead because it cuts down on the length of the weight being used and does not twist around the line.

situations. When fishing fast water with a heavy current be sure to use a fixed weight system that lets you react to the weight. The Slinky is the most effective weight system that you can use when drifting the Klamath River.

The Slinky is simply nylon cord filled with lead

Shore casters fishing for salmon at the mouth of the Klamath. Del Norte Historical Society photo

There is another option used by many fishermen on the river and that is hollow core lead. It is crimped to a dropper of lighter test line than the line being used as leader.

A new invention has revolutionized drift fishing! It tremendously reduces snags and increases the amount of time actually spent fishing, instead of tying knots. This new weight system is the Slinky. Slinky Drifters tend to walk down the crevices and crannys between rocks without any of the snagging problems found with sticky pencil lead. Slinky Drifters can be rigged as sliding sinkers which is recommended in most

pellets and heat sealed. A hole is punched in one end and attached to a free-sliding snap swivel on your main line which is separated from your leader by using a barrel swivel. When casting spinners and using a Slinky, simply tie both main line and leader to the same eye of the snap swivel. There is a debate as to whether or not the Slinky spooks fish. I believe that the Slinky more closely resembles a stick or something natural than does surgical tubing and pencil lead used in the Klamath Cinch. There is also the quiet advantage of having the lead insulated from the loud tap, tap which pencil lead makes while bouncing on the rocks.

Fly Fishing

Fly fishing for steelhead had many of its innovations in California. One of the state's premier rivers is the Klamath, although historically the Eel may have received more national reputation as a fly fishing stream. However, the Klamath has produced its share of fly patterns and famous anglers. Its major tributary, the Trinity, may well be the best steelhead fly fishing stream of them all.

There are many fly patterns that were first tied for use on the Klamath River. Several of these patterns have been widely employed on other rivers in California and elsewhere but for the most part they were local patterns, tied by area anglers who wanted better success.

The Klamath was also a laboratory for the development of fly lines and the late Peter Schwab once thought his quality silk lines would be the fly lines of the future. However it did not happen because synthetics were discovered and have ruled the market over the last 40 years. Today's fly lines cast farther and last longer than any quality silk line could ever hope to.

Flies Of The Klamath

Burlap: First tied for use on the Klamath by Arnold Arana, in 1945. I recently guided his daughter Arlene, who does not fly fish, and her husband, Jim Lazorrotti, a skilled fly caster who can double haul with the greatest of ease. We used the Burlap for summer steelhead fished deep using a Hi-D shooting head.

Brass Hat: One of the flies originated by Peter Schwab of Yreka, California. This fly is said to fish best when the river is off-color.

Brindle Bug: Perhaps the number one fly used on the lower Klamath River. It was first tied about 1955 by the late Lloyd Silvius, owner of a fly shop in Eureka, California. Used both on the Klamath and Trinity, the Brindle Bug is an excellent choice for first fly of the day.

Blue Creek Special: This fly was created in the late 1930s or early 1940s by Bug Bishop of Eureka, California. It is sparsely dressed and understated and is tied upside down with the bucktail under the chenille body in order to turn the hook over. With the hook inverted, it seemed to hook many more steelhead according to Bug Bishop. There is a hackled version that was referred to as the Bug Special by family members and guests of Blue Creek Lodge.

Orleans Barber: Tied by Jim Pray in 1934. Al Kutzkey of Kutzkey Lodge found this to be his favorite fly when fishing the Klamath River, although Al simply referred to it as a grey hackle.

Joe O'Donnel: First tied in the 1930s by an area fly fisherman of the same name, it originated on the midriver area near Orleans.

Pecwan Nymph: First tied by a Washington fly fisherman and imported to the Klamath River in the 1960s. It is fished deep and was first used on the lower Klamath above Johnson's Bar on Mettah Riffle in the Pecwan Creek area.

Queen Bess: This fly was named for Bess Schwab whose husband Peter chronicled her success with the fly. In 1945 he noted that Bess caught a 10-pound steelhead from the Klamath River near the Swallows, their home near Yreka on the Klamath River. It was one of the early experiments with wire bodied flies and gained in notoriety when Schwab's article about it was published in *Sports Afield* in 1946.

Silver Hilton: Named for Henry Hilton whose cabin near Bluff Creek on the Klamath River was also known as Red Rat's Haven. There are two versions of how the fly was named. Local fly historians say it was because of the silver tinsel wrap, however, two of the octogenarians I interviewed said it was named for Mr. Hilton's graying temples which were quite striking. However, an original Silver Hilton tied by Henry Hilton (which I photographed) had no tinsel wrap. Whatever the answer, the Silver Hilton is one of the two most widely used flies on the Klamath River today. First tied in the mid-1940s, the Silver Hilton has kept its popularity among Klamath River fly fishers.

Thor: Despite the fact that this fly received its fame from use on the Eel River, Blue Creek Lodge guides on the Klamath River originally used the Thor almost exclusively. First tied by Jim Pray, Thors for lodge guest use were tied by the lodge's baker, Lloyd Silvius.

Weitchpec Witch: First tied in 1949 this fly remains a favorite in the local area. It bears a close resemblance to the Silver Hilton and may also have been originated by Henry Hilton.

There are many other flies that take steelhead on the Klamath, but the forementioned flies are still some of the best and have survived the test of time. On one of my own guided trips we fished the standard patterns most of the morning and at midday one of the adventurous anglers tied on a Royal Coachman and began to catch steelhead. You never know with steelhead! Fly fishing is rapidly gaining popularity and there is nothing like the fight of a hot 8-pound Klamath River steelhead taking line from your screaming reel. If you have experienced trout on the fly perhaps you are ready to step up to a steelhead. These brutes usually challenge the skills of even the most experienced fly rodders.

Lure Fishing

Methods for taking salmon and steelhead on lures in the Klamath River are many. It is likely that lures take over 50 percent of all the fish caught on the river though no statistics are available. For many years fishing at the mouth of the river for Chinook salmon was done only with lures. According to 82 year old lifetime resident Ed Hughes, anchovies were not fished at the mouth until, "this fellow from Washington came down fishing." It was a slow spinner day and he had brought a new bait with him when he came down the coast. That was how anchovies were first introduced to the fishermen at the mouth. Today spinners still remain the most popular method for fishing the mouth of the river.

Spinners

Many of the spinner designs used by the guides and local sportsmen were made by Vern Flachsman and his wife Ann of Vern's Tackle. He is famous on the lower river for his spinners made both in brass and copper. Vern also made monofilament spreaders for local spinner fishing that gave a spinner fisherman one less knot to break, according to Ron Benedict of Benedict's Tackle. Ron told me that "Ann made the hook action of the spinners firm by wrapping wire around the shank of the hook and the spinner body." This kept the hook from turning when a salmon struck the spinner. The unique figure eight used in securing the hook made for positive hooking without turning found in most ring eye hook setups on spinners.

Ann taught Ron Benedict how to make the

The author at work on the Shasta River at Department of Fish & Games salmon counting station – September, 1982. Beth Burdick photo

spinner patterns that Vern developed and many of these same patterns are still used at the mouth. Ray Benner, who is one of the best lure fishermen in the fishing world today and the cream of the crop of guides that row the mouth of the Klamath River, says that Vern taught him a lot about spinner fishing and that one of Vern's tips was to let the spinner sink to the bottom and rest there a few seconds before moving it – to entice the curious nature of the salmon.

Spinner fishing at the mouth is done with 20 to 40-pound test line on stout rods using stainless steel spring spreaders or one of Vern's monofilament spreaders (still made by Ron Benidict) and enough weight attached to find the bottom. The spinner is pulled against the current created either by outgoing tides or by simply trolling in the estuary immediately above the mouth. In most conditions 3 to 8 ounces of lead is sufficient but at peak tide fluctuations as much as 2 pounds is used. After finding bottom and letting your lure rest, crank in one or two turns and troll the spinner in good looking water. Troll very, very slowly, Chinook like it. Experiment with the depth by varying the number of cranks up from the bottom. Now you are fishing. When you get a bump, fish at that same depth, deeper if it is an incoming tide, shallower if its an outgoing tide.

Remember that the depth changes fairly rapidly in this area of maximum tidal influence.

As the fish leave tidewater and begin their journey upriver, there are large concentrations of bank and boat anglers casting hardware of virtually every variety. If one lure was to be pointed out as the most popular, it would be the Mepps, in size No. 3 with a silver blade. Most of the spinners are fished with weight attached to the line to obtain the depth necessary for catching salmon and steelhead. It will undoubtedly cost you some lures, but it's a price well worth paying and should decrease as you learn the river's snags and holding water. When you begin fishing spinners, each and every day vary your rate of retrieve, stop sometimes, buzz it on the surface, keep changing until you find the motion that is working on that day. It's a fact that some days the fish will be overly aggressive and follow a speedy lure and smash it. Other days the same fish might follow the lure and not strike it until it stops, falls to the bottom and begins to move again. Some days fish barely bump the lures, demanding from you a touch comparable to bait fishing in order to catch a fish. Always experiment each day and you will be more successful fishing with spinners on the river.

In the upper river many anglers use spinners for winter steelheading. Long time spinner fisherman Joe Clyburn prefers Rooster Tails: black for muddy water, yellow for in-between and red on brown in clear water. "Of course, I don't always catch a fish," chuckles Joe as he remains humble in spite of his having fished the area all of his life – a mere 78 years! I've watched Joe on winter mornings when I needed to warm my reel hand and stopped fishing. His quick, accurate casts varied in angles as he covered the entire drift in front of him. He would snap the Rooster Tail across the river, click the bail on his spinning reel, and let the current take the spinner down and across until it caught and started spinning; then lowered his rod tip and begin a slow retrieve. Joe never attaches weight to his Rooster Tails, he always fishes the spinner straight, no weight. I've seen that rodtip quiver as Joe reared back on another steelhead. Each and every fish Joe catches on his spinner is carefully examined and if there is any color to it Joe releases it and returns to casting until he finds one he feels is fresh enough to take home to Lucille! I've never seen Joe keep more than one fish unless he had a particular person already in mind to take one to. Spinners are very effective throughout the Klamath River and are also one of the best choices when fishing for spring salmon in May and June.

Ernie Halton displays a limit of spring chinook. Limits at that time were two adults (over 22") and three jacks (under 22") daily. Bette Halton photo

Plugs

The use of diving plugs throughout the river to catch steelhead is very popular today among drift boaters in the middle and upper portions of the river and some jet boaters in the lower river. The two plugs that are most commonly used are the Hot Shot and Wee Wart. The Klamath River is one of the first places pulling plugs was perfected by upriver guides. Al Kutzkey and Jim Roads are the avowed former masters of drift boat fishing. Their popularization of the back trolling method for taking winter steelhead has spread and today it's a common method employed by almost all serious guides and anglers.

If one color of plug is to be designated best for the Klamath River, it would be yellow. In the standard green water of winter steelhead fishing it's been the favorite color of virtually every guide present and past. In clear water, silver and black or silver and blue are the two most common colors used.

The key to fishing plugs is to cover all of the likely holding water that you can in a day. That way you have more of an opportunity to put the plug in front of a fish. Today's avowed master of plug fishing, Ray Benner, explains that fish have three reactions when they are presented with a plug; one, to go around the plug, two, to drop back downriver, or three, to grab the plug. If they do one or three you're either into or out of a fish, but if the fish drops back your continual dropping of the plug down the same slot can elicit a reluctant steelhead to take the plug.

A new method for taking fish on Wee Warts was discovered by one of the local anglers in Klamath last year. There were schools of silver salmon rolling in the frog water between holes and they refused offerings of bait. Attaching a flame Wee Wart to 36 inches of leader and pencil lead held in a Klamath Cinch he simply cast and retrieved through the rolling fish. It is quite effective and by year's end nearly every guide on the river had his customers casting these gaudy plugs to catch the silvers. Some days it was so effective that barbless hooks were used to release the silvers unharmed.

Jigs

The most common jig fished in the Klamath River is the Kast Master and it is not fished in the traditional method one associates with jigging. It is usually fished by cast and retrieve or by top line trolling (without any weight attached) in the estuary. Jigging however is very effective when dealing with suspended fish that are holding in the in-between depths and not near the bottom. Kast Masters and Krocodiles fished in the slow, deep water will sometimes reward an angler with larger than average salmon. It is certainly true that jigs and spinners take some of the largest salmon every year. True jigging is a technique yet to be popularized on the Klamath.

Bait Fishing

Commonly called drift fishing among steelheaders, the subtle finesse of detecting a bite when fishing bait has been over-mystified by teachers when attempting to share their ability with new students of the sport. There is one fact to remember when you are a beginner learning how to bait fish for salmonids. For every bite you actually receive there will be numerous pauses, pulsations, stops, grabs by vicious rocks, hook-ups with lost rigs of other fishermen and every other fish-like sensation imaginable. If your teacher takes a smug attitude telling you, "I can always tell a bite from a snag, I never miss a bite" or any such absolute claims, quickly dismiss it as bragging. Do not become frustrated, confused or dubious! Follow simply rules and remember each spot in the water you are fishing where you received a bite sensation. In the formations found on the river bottom there are many things that feel like a bite even to a veteran steelheader. By learning the water from repeated fishing trips or numerous casts, the experts quite simply gain a home-court advantage. Many novices, when bait fishing, have the problem of waiting for a bite and are continually jerking off their bait with snappy hook sets. When you are learning to bait fish or anytime you are unsure what is going on at the other end of your line, lift quickly with your whole arm, taking up the slack. If you feel any weight or resistance you will still have plenty of hook setting ability left from your elbow on down. Don't get snag shy! If you feel weight, SET THE HOOK! It is in the initial motion that you should learn to lift and not to jerk. After you fish an individual piece of water enough times, you will know every bump and grab of the bottom and look just like one of those old time experts who have been telling you that it is a skill some have and some don't. It's a skill that everyone can learn.

Cured roe is the most effective bait on a day to day basis for both salmon and steelhead throughout the entire Klamath River system. Although a few fishermen, mostly in the upper river, still use roe tied in moaline sacks that they call berries, the vast majority of roe is simply fished using a roe loop to hold pieces of cured bait onto the back of the hook. An additional attractor is often used with the roe. Some of the most common are styrofoam drift balls (made locally in Crescent City), Spin 'N Glos, Corkies, Birdy Drifters and colored yarn. Bank anglers throughout the river take many fish on roe drift fished in the riffles. Boat anglers usually move the bait through the hole by drifting with the current and casting the bait upstream, dragging it behind the boat. Though often called boondoggling there is a difference. In true boondoggling the boat and bait drift through different currents, actually side drifting the bait in an attempt to avoid the boat's spooking the fish. (This is something I've been working earnestly on perfecting for steelhead in the shallow riffles throughout the lower Klamath.) Any of the attractors can also be used to catch fish without any roe at all. A good example of this was a day I remember well on the Shasta River; I was literally buried by a young boy and his father using small Okie Drifters. They continually caught fish and my fresh roe went through the same water untouched. It was a humbling experience for me in my education about the change that's required to be successful on a regular basis as a steelhead fisherman.

Glo Bug

The popularity of Glo Bugs, a round yarn ball similar to a large salmon egg, is growing every year. There are many who prefer the no-mess of a Glo Bug and simply add scent for attraction. When fishing with Glo Bugs you are also sure that you have something attractive to fish on your hook at all times. There are also many days when Glo Bugs will out-fish roe for steelhead. I've seen it proven time and time again although roe is still more effective for salmon than Glo Bugs. There are two colors predominantly used: baby pink and orange. For best results use orange early in the day or as long as it's overcast; use pink when the sun is on the water. This is a general rule. I've noticed some start their morning with both colors on different rods and as soon as the first fish is caught they switch all the rods to that color. It makes a lot of sense to find out what is working and then go with it. If you fish the Klamath River for steelhead be sure to try Glo Bugs, my favorite bait for steelhead.

The Extended Drift

One of the best techniques for taking steelhead and salmon on bait when drift fishing from the bank is by extending your drift. When you get done with the normal routine of making a drift and your bait swings into the slot, the seam between currents, you can use a level wind reel to cover more water and long line your bait on free spool right to waiting fish. It's one of the tricks Ernie Hatton taught a group of younger bankies, including John Bergamo who achieved a fine touch when extending his drift and has become one of the finest bank anglers on the lower Klamath River. In 1989 John caught a 15½ pound steelhead on the lower Klamath River.

Today's Opportunities

When introducing the newcomer to salmon and steelhead fishing it's necessary to explain that today's advancements in tackle and line have greatly reduced the labor and skill required to become a competent angler. Many frustrations such as tangles, break-offs, backlashes and other headaches have been eliminated from modern fishing. If you've had a bad experience fishing in the past or have been putting off learning how to become a skilled angler, then now is the time to learn. If you have left your piscatorial pursuits behind because of the once dwindling supply of fish in our rivers and the many hours required to catch one, now is the time to pick up your rod. Runs of salmon and steelhead are rebuilding. Now is the time for our focus to remain on the rebuilding of anadromous stocks. The all time low populations of the late 1970s and early 1980s have been enhanced and recovery is apparent on the Klamath River.

Reading Water

Drifting is the most common method of bait fishing on the Klamath River and can be done from the bank or from a floating or anchored boat. Salmon and steelhead are moving through the river on their spawning migration. As they ascend the river they use great amounts of energy and they follow the path of least resistance. Logically, heavy, strong, currented water will slow down the fish. Usually they will rest at the head of, or just above, the riffle. Start there, remember to vary your casts and work all of the water with a systematic approach.

Every riffle has particular areas that hold fish. After repeated fishing trips, these will become known to you and you will be able to concentrate on them as you move through the rest of the water quickly while still covering it all. When the run is in fish will almost constantly be on the move in fast, riffled water, but the hot spots will be areas where fish can pause to rest while exerting less energy than in the majority of the riffle. Always pay close attention to the seams where the fast current and the slower water meet near the edge. This is the usual path that the majority of migrating salmon and steelhead take. For fish less strain is more gain on their spawning migration.

Often the water temperature of the Klamath River in the summer and fall reaches 68 to 73 degrees. During this period the fish seek the cool relief of deep water and you will find concentrations of fish in the holes. In the lower Klamath River the fish hold longest at the mouth of Blue Creek which is one of the few streams with enough water flow to make a significant change in the river's temperature. I have recorded temperature differences of as much as 8 degrees between the river above the mouth and immediately below the creek. There are years when early season fishing is concentrated at the mouth of Blue Creek as fish literally stop migrating and stack up while waiting for cooler water temperatures.

Reading water is essential to becoming consistently productive when salmon and steelhead fishing. There is nothing more important than fishing the water that holds the fish, after all, even the best angler cannot catch fish when beating empty waters.

Tackle

RODS

SALMON – In order to gear up with the heavier test lines that are used when fishing the mouth, a stout rod and large capacity reel are required. A rod suited for 20 to 40-pound test has the necessary backbone for handling a large salmon in close quarters. There are numerous fine rods on the market. I will not endorse brands here, only point out that you need to know in advance of buying a rod, what is to be expected of it when fishing.

STEELHEAD – Almost all of the light to medium-weight steelhead rods provide the sensitive action necessary to distinguish the subtlest of bites and provide the power to handle any steelhead and most of the salmon on the Klamath River (except at the mouth). I suggest an 8-foot rod with a sensitive rod tip rated for 6 to 12-pound test. This will provide plenty of reach for playing a fish around a boat or for banking a frisky steelhead.

REELS

While I've often heard the suggestion of spending your money and buying the best, there are some people who either cannot afford it, or question the investment when they are not sure how much they will enjoy and pursue fishing. If you are going to skimp, do it in the cost of a rod and not in the cost of a reel. Buy the best reel available and know its value as a tool. It will reward you even when you step up to a better rod. I suggest you buy a Shimano level wind reel. The one area that I've clearly seen the advantage in one product over the other has been the reels. Shimano level wind reels are the number one choice for fishing throughout salmon and steelhead country. I have several and some have landed hundreds of salmon and steelhead without missing a single cast. They have out performed every other reel I've bought and some were much more expensive. Today's level wind reels are also easy to learn to cast! Don't be intimidated by stories of backlashes because these reels are products of advanced technology and compensate for your errors in casting.

6 Recent History

Throughout its history, the Klamath River has lived up to its claim of being the salmon and steelhead capital of California! During the 1980s, the Klamath River has been the best place to catch, not just fish for, salmon and steelhead in the state of California. Steelhead populations have outnumbered all other rivers in the state and salmon populations are on the rise, pointing to a better fishery each year. With the future an optimistic one, still some controls are necessary for the continued improvement of the Klamath River's fishery.

Quotas

Salmon have always been precious to each user group and Klamath River salmon are divided each year between commercial ocean trollers, ocean sportsmen, the Indian gill-net harvest, and river sport anglers. Severe cutbacks in the ocean troll have allowed for two consecutive years, 1986 and 1987, of stock rebuilding. The Pacific Fisheries Management Council and the State Fish and Game Commission make the ultimate decisions as to the actual division of the fish. There have been years, such as 1988's ocean sport catch, that anglers have caught too many fish too fast and normal daily limits of two adult salmon had to be reduced to one salmon per day. This quota system has also been accompanied by California's first punch card (although the punch card only applies to the Klamath River basin, including the Trinity River and the Pacific Ocean inside the Klamath Management Zone).

The daily limit for adult salmon is two over 22 inches. Under the punch card system, each angler is allowed six adult salmon in any seven consecutive days. This is an attempt to both spread out and prolong the harvest so the quota is not reached too quickly. The punch card was also a preferred option over the previous years of 1984 and 1985 when sport fishermen had to suffer Monday and Tuesday closures.

Increased Limit

Another big change involved in the new punch-card system is each anglers' daily allowed limit. Instead of the previous three fish, no more than two of which could be salmon, the daily bag limit increased to five salmon, no more than two over 22 inches. In addition to the five salmon, anglers are allowed to keep three steelhead. This makes for an incredible limit of eight fish per angler daily. This liberal limit should keep anglers from abusing any of the Department of Fish and Game's regulations.

Fish And Wildlife

One of the major studies being conducted by the USDFW (U.S.Department of Fish and Wildlife) takes place at the mouth of the Klamath River. USDFW biologists operate a seine net there for collection and tagging of fall Chinook salmon. This study is being funded by the

Bureau of Indian Affairs in order to collect data on fish populations and migration timing.

Collecting the salmon by use of a 100-meter seine net, USDFW crew members hand-net the salmon and place them in live tanks where they are momentarily held until they can be measured and tagged with jaw tags. Next the salmon are revived by crew members and returned to their spawning journey – hopefuly to have the tags recovered upstream by anglers, at counting stations or hatcheries.

Located at the mouth of the river amidst the crowds of fishermen and tourists, the net crew has become one of the local tourist attractions. There has also been controversy pro and con about the project and the fact that it leaves so very many stressed salmon in the most pressured area of predation by gill nets, hooks and lines and most importantly, seals and sea lions.

USDFW also monitors the juvenile populations of downstream migrants throughout the Klamath River drainage.

Department Of Fish And Game

There are many projects currently being undertaken by CDFG (California Department of Fish and Game) on the Klamath River and its tributaries. These include a lower river seine site to tag migrating species, creel census personal who record sport catch statistics of river angling, counting stations (weirs) on all of the major tributaries, carcass surveys (water level allowing) to estimate spawning populations, and the operation of two hatcheries. One is located on the Klamath at Iron Gate Dam and the other on the Trinity at Lewiston Dam. There are also plans for another CDFG hatchery on the Shasta River near Big Springs.

The policy of DFG in California has placed the emphasis on Chinook salmon, no doubt because of their commercial value to the fishing industry. This raises a question of value with many anglers including myself. When it is the licensed angler whose fees support the department, why does so much of the budget and the fish it produces go to commercial ocean trollers? What about steelhead? It is time for sport anglers to work together to insure they receive equal representation in CDFG's future management. It's time to change the department back to a resource agency instead of a fish farm for commercial ocean fishermen. People want more steelhead and less bureaucracy from CDFG.

U.S. Fish & Wildlife crew running the siene net for tagging at the mouth of the Klamath. George Burdick photo

Project Fish

The California Department of Fish and Game has ignored steelhead. In this time of rebuilding salmon runs and hatchery production geared almost entirely towards salmon, mid-river fishermen have suffered the most. In this portion of the river,traditionally a steelhead mecca, salmon spend little time. The majority of their river time is spent in the lower portions of the river or in the headwaters, near or at the mouths of major spawning tributaries where they linger long enough to provide a viable fishery.

Now something is being done by a coalition composed of area river guides, Karok Indians, the U.S. Forest Service and, at length, CDFG. Much of the credit for organizing this effort should go to Al Foss, longtime guide and at 71 years of age, anxious to see steelhead return to the Klamath. The answer is project F.I.S.H., which stands for Fish Improvement Steelhead Hatchery. Plans are underway for a three tank (3,000 gallons each) hatchery located in the midriver near Bluff Creek. The Sacramento

Valley Tomato Growers donated the tanks for raising steelhead. The water source is 150 GPM and everyone involved is optimistic about success.

When I interviewed Al Foss the legal agreement between groups was in the signature stage. Hopefully, selective breeding of steelhead will bring back remnants of the old Bluff Creek steelhead, known for their size and fighting strength. The Forest Service is providing the site, the Karok Indians are financing and helping with construction and operation, guides are donating labor and funds and CDFG is supplying eggs and feed for the juvenile steelhead reared at the hatchery. Working free, as legal counsel for project F.I.S.H., is attorney Phil Smith, owner of the Bluff Creek Store.

This is a five year project with hopes of creating a turn around in three years, four at most. Plans call for production to eventually supply steelhead juveniles to plant the entire Klamath River. Funds are needed and with time and cooperation project F.I.S.H. will soon be a reality.

Fish Rescue

Each season the receding waters of the spring run-off leave behind anadromous offspring swimming downstream, ever seaward. Juvenile salmon and steelhead are caught in puddles that leave them without oxygen. Fisheries organizations are presently active in fish rescue. It's very satisfying to see the fish you save swim away. Some of the fish rescue projects have even included rearing of the young fish before eventual release.

Present Timing Of Runs

If you decide upon the Klamath River as a destination for your vacation, there are several distinct areas, each different in climate, terrain, vegetation and timing for the best fishing opportunities. The single most important factor in planning a successful trip is to arrive when there are fish in the river. Every year many people pass through the resort I stay at and voice their dismay that they didn't come when the fishing was good.

There is one sure month for the lower Klamath River and that is September. There are always plenty of salmon and steelhead throughout the lower river in September. Though very crowded the fishing is definitely worth enduring the boats and people. There is usually a friendly camaraderie among anglers and many good times are shared. Everyone catches fish in September on the lower Klamath River.

The fishing season and the yearly cycle of anadromous runs begins with the spring run of Chinook salmon that starts in April and lasts through July. There are many peaks and valleys in this run and fishing can be alternately rewarding and disappointing due to the springers' rapid migration. Most of the fishing occurs in the Trinity River or the lower Klamath River. During this same period of time summer steelhead also begin to ascend the Klamath. A few fish work their way upriver each month but during July there is usually a very strong run both in fish size and numbers. This is one of my favorite times to fish the river because there are quality days, explosive steelhead, fat spring salmon and very few boats on the river.

August is the turning point between spring and fall-run Chinook. As the major run of salmon enters the Klamath, the crowds of anglers that pursue them reaches its peak. Steelhead also keep coming into the river during August and the cycle of the Klamath's famous half-pounder run enters the river in full swing, with cycles of two good years followed by two bad ones. By August, fishing action is working its way up the river as fish migrations bring schools through each riffle and pool. September is the peak; there is a frenzy of fishing action that fills R.V. parks and swells the river from the bulk of the lead cast into it by thousands of anglers. To an individual who first views this rite of fall fishing frenzy it must seem inconceivable that so many anglers can crowd so closely together – flailing long rods, heavy weights and sharp hooks – at the mouth of the Klamath. Labor Day weekend the crowd peaks. In September there are salmon passing through virtually every portion of the river you choose to fish. Usually the first numbers of salmon arrive at Iron Gate Hatchery in mid-month and September is also the peak fish-count month at the Shasta River Weir which is 175 miles upriver.

October can provide good coho fishing on the lower portion of the river and is usually the dividing time between summer and winter-run steelhead. In every winter month there are runs of steelhead entering the river bound for different upriver tributaries. When not muddy, the Klamath can be a very good winter steelhead river, though most of the fish are smaller than those in the Eel or Smith rivers. Most mid and upriver guides and lodges book the majority of their trips for winter steelhead, fished by drift boat, from November to February.

According to many CDFG biologists who know the Klamath, there are fish entering the river every month of the year. In the winter runs of large steelhead enter the lower Klamath River, often they are bound for small creeks that only run in winter and a short period of the spring and then dry up in summer. Steelhead in the 10 to 20-pound range are common but California's winter rains generally render the river unfishable.

Wild Mountain Lily. Joe B. Clyburn photo

Tributaries

Trinity River: The most important and largest tributary of the Klamath River. In fact on many of the early maps of the Klamath area, the mainstem of the Klamath River below the confluence was labeled as the Trinity River. Its clear, cool waters are a contrast to the slightly green nutrient rich waters of the Klamath. At the head of the river, Lewiston Dam and hatchery mark the end of upstream migration. Current outstanding populations of both salmon and steelhead have made the Trinity River's popularity among anglers a recent phenomenon. The much smaller Trinity has more salmon than the entire remaining Klamath River including the Salmon, Scott and Shasta rivers. In 1987, there were 91,000 adult fall Chinook salmon counted in the Trinity River. Additionally, the spring salmon run has become a good fishery throughout the river and in 1988, it was estimated at 50,000 Chinook.

Many guides specialize in fly fishing for steelhead on the Trinity which is one of the most productive steelhead fly fishing rivers in California. Of the current guides operating in the area, Herb Burton, outdoor writer and long time guide, is referred to by United Anglers of California as the "best guide on the Trinity River." His articles have appeared in many fishing news publications as well as *Salmon Trout Steelheader* magazine. Herb rows the river in a raft while most guides prefer to use a drift boat for their clients comfort. A good place to call for information concerning fishing on the Trinity is Brady's Bait 'n Tackle, Weaverville, California.

There are many major restoration projects underway on the Trinity. The objectives are to restore the fishery and improve existing facilities throughout the river. This also includes funding of the Trinity River Flow Evaluation Study which will determine an annual flow pattern to encourage migration, spawning, rearing and the flushing flows needed for downstream migrants.

This restoration will cost 57 million dollars with 50 percent of the funding being paid by the Central Valley Water Project. (Water from the Trinity is pumped over the mountains and shipped to users in the Sacramento Valley.) The minimum flow requirements, once agreed upon with the aid of the Klamath Trinity Coalition, are subject to re-evaluation under this program.

River restoration will also include construction of Buckhorn Dam. The reason stated for building the dam is to prevent decomposed granite sediment from destroying fish habitat in the Trinity River. This is part of the continuing problem caused by placer gold mines that once operated there.

Salmon River

This crystalline river is as close to a wilderness fishing experience in a primitive setting as can be found in the state. It is accessible by road, though a one lane, hair pin highway follows the river on a scary route alongside granite cliffs that fall away 1,000 feet or more to the river below. It is not a road for the weak of heart, but is worth the experience.

Salmon River Canyon is a hard-rock, quick-fall area strewn with granite boulders and heavy rapids. It is becoming increasingly popular with rafters and kayakers and has several Class V rapids. The huge Nordheimer slide has made a great fall that is fun for rafters but a strain for migrating salmon and steelhead. Despite being blown by CDFG it is still quite an obstruction for migrating fish.

Its crystal clear water more closely resembles that of the Smith River rather than one of the Klamath's tributaries. An article in *Flyfishing* magazine, by Marty Sherman, expressed the virtues of a remote setting combined with the fine steelhed fly fishing he found at Otter Bar Lodge. Currently the Salmon River is being referred to as Cal Salmon to distinguish it from Idaho's better known Salmon River.

Scott River

Some of my fondest memories are of winter steelhead fishing in Scott Valley near Fort Jones. The small size of the river made for a pleasant drift on a winter day. There were rarely any other boats and the quiet solitude is something I'll always cherish. (If you decide to drift the Scott, access is very limited. I had a key to a farmer's gate to launch. Also beware, the canyon area below Scott Valley is not driftable water and you should take out just below the Quartz Valley Bridge on the left hand bank as you are floating downstream.) I also remember the days when the fog hung thick in the small mountain valley and the moisture clung to the trees freezing each limb in an icy vision of white. The Scott has a good population of steelhead and is a good bet for bank anglers who want to get away from it all. The entire 30 miles of canyon below the Scott valley is rarely fished and is often productive.

U.S. Forest Service raft flips in Last Chance Rapids on the Salmon River. Rower Dave Atwood U.S.F.S. Ranger. Steve Riede photo

Shasta River

This is the most studied of all the Klamath River tributaries. The Shasta River is still a major spawning stream for fall-run Chinook. Shasta River Weir counters have kept track of spawning numbers since 1930 and from the historical fluctuations in populations it is easy to understand the decline of the fishery. (See Table 5, Chapter 3.) The river reached its historical low during the mid-1980s, but more recent years show that there has been an end to the decline and reason for optimism about the future of our salmon runs.

The author passes another salmon from the trap, upstream to spawn. Beth Burdick photo

Also CDFG has been building gabions (rock barriers) to trap gravel that has been hauled in to make spawning beds. Gravel depletion is of concern in all upper river areas and should not be overlooked in rebuilding efforts.

My former wife, Beth, and I worked for CDFG at the Shasta River Weir counting salmon and steelhead. We were on our way to town, driving the windy highway that follows the Shasta River, when I chanced to see two men standing waist deep in the spawning beds behind the gabions. Stopping, we saw yellow ropes in their hands attached to grappling hooks. We drove upriver and across to the dirt road access on the old Shasta Highway to gain a closer look. Near the snaggers we grew wary and I sent Beth to town to call the warden. While crouching behind their car I let the air out of the two outside tires. When finished, I walked down the road certain that what I had done was just. It would also make the warden's job much easier. As it turned out the two men were wanted in Redding for armed robberies and were bonafide bad guys.

I've always been too over-zealous when protecting our fisheries from abuse. I've paid for my actions and suffered some physical damage due to my beliefs. I am still a hard head and think if more of us truly cared we would at least take the time to stand up for our natural heritage to these rapists of our resources. California is currently being plagued by Vietnamese who are adept at illegal hoop netting. They have been active in the Pacific Ocean, San Francisco Bay, the Delta, and Sacramento, Russian, and Eel rivers. This is illegal netting of our precious fish and to a Vietnam veteran, a real mind inflaming situation. I can only urge the department responsible for enforcement to bring this problem to a quick and immediate end.

Ethics, Manners And Safety

I would be remiss in writing this book without educating novice boaters, anglers and even guides as to the rules of the road for fishing on any river as well as the particular practices of courtesy normally observed on the Klamath River.

The Klamath is a long river of moderate flow and will accommodate many boats and fishermen if all observe common sense, the basic rights of others and approach the river as a social/scenic outing that certainly involves seeing other people. I always think about the first trip I took to Alaska's Kenai River, only to find it more crowded in Alaska than it was on the Klamath. If you want to have the river to yourself, salmon and steelhead fishing should not be your sport. Conditions are only going to become increasingly crowded and learning to fish with other people while having fun doing so is essential to the quality of our angling experience.

The right of way when boating should always be given to any boat not under power, such as drift boats, rafts or any boat ahead of you when passing through narrow channels. When fishing, any person with a fish on should be accorded first rights and those fishing or boating should yield their positions by reeling in and getting out of the way. Also, in fishing there is a basic rule of first come, first served although there are times when manners dictate that the first comer should adjust his position or style of fishing in order to enable other anglers to also fish the water. I am referring to situations where you are first to a drift and have anchored up in order to fish. Then a number of bank anglers arrive and you are obviously in the way, but by moving your position everyone gets to fish.

Boat Ethics

When fishing from a drift boat, while pulling plugs or bait divers, you spend your entire day fishing water downstream. The water below you is what you are fishing through and should not be taken away by other boaters passing and setting up in front of your boat on the same side of the river! Never drop below another boat and begin fishing in the same run whether it is 100 feet or 200 feet downstream. That is water to avoid out of courtesy. You can set up on the other side of the river or wait until the boat in front of you is done with the run. It would surprise you how many times you can fish behind another boat and catch fish.

Author with a 10-pound salmon. Marv Cooper photo

I have my own theory about this phenomenon. After fish move to avoid the other boat, often not even seeing or responding to their offering, they are more likely to expend the energy to strike, bite or attack the second boat's plugs, baits or flies. It has happened so many times I often use the tactic and drop anchor to let another boat stir the pot. I have also been burnt by this method and sat while watching them play a fish.

Always fish carefully and remember that the Klamath River has some very active white water, several Class IIs and IIIs, a few IVs and, of course, Ishi Pishi Falls. The river can over-power you. The key is setting up before you enter the rapids.

Boating safety normally includes life preservers, fire extinguisher, first aid kit, oars for motor boats or a third oar for drift boats, anchor and tool kit. I also like to add 100 feet of rope to that list, especially in a drift boat on water that is new to me. Choosing safe water to fish, knowing your skill level and always scouting unknown drifts are also part of safe boating. There is a common weak spot among anglers and boaters, a moment when we become obsessed and expose our achilles heel rendering us vulnerable to poor judgement – that's when we are playing a fish! I've seen people at the mouth of the Klamath try to follow a large salmon to sea rather than observe the safety rules. When the Coast Guard operator clamped on to their boat, they were screaming, "our fish, our fish!" I saw a guide of some experience trap a downstream oar on his drift boat while trying to net a client's fish and almost roll his drift boat. I've seen bank anglers follow a fish to a cut bank and jump into the river rather than be spooled, waders and all. There are many accidents that happen while fishing that could have been avoided by forethought. Remember accidents happen quickly! Proper preparation and caution can go a long way in lowering the vulnerability for each of us.

One growing habit among owners of larger boats on the lower Klamath is the practice of taxiing between drifts in order to avoid putting water from their wakes into smaller boats and to keep from stirring up the hole and making it hard to fish for everyone. It is often crowded and a wait is necessary before you take your turn drifting through a hole anyway. When there is a tourist or visiting guide who doesn't catch on to the system everyone is quick to point out why we taxi. Of course there are a few who never will change the way they fish on the river and seem to have their head in the clouds. It is also the same one or two guides without manners who cause problems year in and year out.

Another point I'd like to discuss is the attitude people take with them to the river – impatience and loss of everyday civilities are common on the river. Instead of viewing other anglers as competitors and even invaders who are intruding on your fishing hole, you might want to adjust your thinking to one of tolerance. Pristine wilderness fishing does not happen on boatable waters of the Klamath River. Scenic and relaxing, social and sharing are the types of fishing experiences left for us today.

Ethics are always debatable and subject to opinions that differ from person to person. Hopefully there can be some agreement on issues such as: litter and cleaning up the water quality, peeing in the river, changing your oil in the river (an inboard owner did that this year on the Klamath), and abusing the limits set by the state – including the stockpiling of fish!

It's hard not to have compassion for retired people who depend on the fish that they can freeze and smoke to supplement their fixed incomes. Yet there are still too many who abuse the resource! We need education, conscience raising and the practice of catch and release. Hopefully, the CDFG will adopt a statewide punch-card system that includes an annual limit for salmon and steelhead. Because of its nature and setting amid an area of gill-net fishing, a general attitude of who can get the most is common on the lower river.

The Race Question

It's been very enlightening to do research for this book. When I first went to the local museum, I couldn't understand why there were so many pictures of Indian woman and very few of Indian men. As I got further into the family trees of the local clans, I found that many of them were the offspring of European immigrants who took Indian women for wives. Names like Patapoff, a Russian name, Sanderson, a Swedish name, Haberman, a German name, and the fact that they had offspring with Indian wives mixed the races.

Today, three generations later, the mixing of blood has thinned the pure Indian to almost extinction. Almost all of the families have white blood or are actually more white than Indian. The fact that the equation for Indian rights includes Indians who are only one-thirty-second seems to me to be carrying Indian rights to an obscure point where it is hard to tell who the Indians are. I asked a young local boy who is one-eighth Indian what he thought he was, white or Indian? He quickly replied, Indian and denied his white blood. Indian today in Klamath is often more an attitude rather than in the blood lines of its people.

Terry Whiteberg with a steelhead caught on a Brindal Bug. Chuck Hammersted photo

I have mixed feelings but in my heart I know the Indians will never have equality until they assimilate and enter society, leaving the reservation behind forever. The romantic side of me, however, knows that this has so long been the homeland of the Indians that they truly belong here. The quiet redwood paradise they once had is now only a memory of the past.

River Happenings

On October 10, 1985 a 16-foot, 4,000-pound great white shark washed up on the beach at Dad's Camp. It was very dead, but also a sobering reminder to the surfers who often find good waves just off the mouth of the Klamath. When salmon gather for their river spawning run, seals and sea lions congregate to chase and eat the salmon, and great white sharks gather to feast upon the seals. It is a nervous place for wet suit clad surfers who look similar to a seal. (While I proofed this book a surfer was attacked by a great white shark requiring 28 stitches from the 14-inch bite.)

On October 12, 1985, I was fortunate enough to hook, fight and land an IGFA line-class, world-record sturgeon from the Klamath River. It was 68 pounds, 4 ounces and was caught on 10-pound Trilene which is rated at 8 kilo (16 pound) on the international breaking-strength scale. It is the only world record fish ever recorded by a Klamath River angler.

Author with I.G.F.A. world record sturgeon 10-12-85. Marv Cooper photo

Flood

In the winter of 1986, the river reached flood stage and the backwater closed Highway 101 just north of the river. Some stock was stranded, but everything was quickly back to normal. This was the only flood of consequence since 1964.

Derby

Annual Have-A-Heart Derby, is held every Labor Day weekend as a benefit for the Heart Association. Prizes, trophies and a barbecue are all part of the derby. Awards are given for first through third place for salmon and steelhead. It is very crowded on the busiest weekend of the year, but it is a fun time, full of friendly competition.

Requa Queen jet boat tours were brought back in 1988. This is an upriver boat ride for those who desire to see the more remote areas upstream from the town of Klamath. There are no public roads in the area and the only public access is by water.

In 1988, cutbacks in the federal budget caused the Coast Guard station at the mouth of the Klamath River to close and river safety has been left entirely up to the Sheriff's Department.

Salmon Festival

For the past 22 years, during the first weekend in August, Native Americans, Klamath residents and tourists gather together to celebrate the annual return of migrating fall Chinook salmon. A traditional barbecue of salmon cooked on redwood stakes over an open alder fire begins each year's festivities. This Indian style salmon is some of the best you will ever eat. The town also gathers for logging contests, traditional Indian dances and many open booth attractions – emanating a carnival atmosphere.

Each year we are reminded of the wonders of our West Coast's great anadromous salmonid runs. The return of the salmon and the important place it holds in the history of Klamath is a fine cause for celebration. Now we can also celebrate the working together of all the river user groups and the fact that we have had better returns in the last two years. Continued cooperation is the reason for this return of our amazing salmon. I can think of few better reasons to gather together in celebration.

A True Fish Story

In October of 1987 while fishing with Mark Sanderson and Marv Cooper, we hooked into a very active steelhead in the 10- pound range. Marv's rod bent double as the leaps and cartwheels of a chrome bright fish quickly changed into an explosive run away from the boat. I quickly realized that the drag on the spinning reel had frozen and wasn't paying out any line. Leaping to action from behind the console of my jet sled, I took the rod from Marv's hands and threw the bail open on the spinning reel allowing line to run freely. I yelled to Mark to break the rigging off his rod and quickly wrapped the slack line pulled from the reel around Marv's hand. Breaking the line at the rod tip, I used a triple surgeons knot to mend the two ends of the monofilament line together then handed back to Marv a jumping, thrashing, 10-pound steelhead on a new rod and reel. Unfortunately Marv lost the fish about two minutes later, keeping the feat from being a complete act of fishing's lore and legend.

The Future

It was very apparent in the low water, drought year of 1988 that central and southern portions of California were eying the Klamath/Trinity basin as a source for future water needs. Plans set forth for a system of dams throughout the Klamath River are on hold and I've had assurances from many sources that these dams will not be built in my lifetime. This puts the focus of responsibility on future generations to protect the integrity of the river and its fisheries by never allowing these dams to be built. It is not a pressing current issue, but one that lies dormant waiting to be put into motion in the future. It will probably be necessary for our children and their children to work continually to preserve the Klamath River. I'd rather they put astro turf on the ten million back yards in Southern California than use the water for lawns. There are many ways to cut water use rather than spoil nature. One sixth of all the water that flows into the Pacific Ocean in the state of California does so in tiny Del Norte County. It is a valuable item, water, and is at the center of development for the state. The population and votes are in the South. It is the legacy of free flowing rivers that they should remain to provide the necessary contrast between the world we have built and the natural world that has always been our passage to relaxation and release.

Keeping the water comes first, but maintaining healthy populations of fish and providing sensible harvest limits on all user groups based on the supply is also important. User groups sometimes maintain that this division has been poorly managed and say that there is an abundance of salmon. I do not agree and maintain that although the Klamath River has had better numbers in 1986 and 1987, they still are far below historic levels. We should not let a small gain turn our heads and change the direction of harvest quotas. Only by keeping adequate escapement stocks can we totally rebuild our fisheries.

At a meeting of commercial fishermen with the Fish and Game Commission, I heard some commercial fishermen state outlandish opinions such as: "There were so many salmon in the Klamath River in 1987 that you could walk across the river on their backs and never touch bottom," "Shasta River isn't able to support more than 2,000 spawning adult salmon" and that we have "more fish in every river in the state than we need." All of which are totally false. In that same meeting I heard many angry fishermen whom want more fish now for their own profit, but few who voiced concern for rebuilding projects or ideas for improving the resource. The entire meeting was spent voicing selfish demands for immediate fish. If commercial fishermen took control of their own future and promoted massive fishery enhancement and restocking, and spent their money to raise fish instead of raise objections we would see a turn around in our salmon runs and have reason to praise their efforts. The more I get involved in the logistics of fish and fishing, the more I resent user group demands upon the fishery without those same groups responding by improving the situation.

It can all be summed up in the quotation from the 1960s: "If you are not part of the solution then you are part of theproblem." As a country capable of space flight, putting a man on the moon and even capable of destroying the entire world instantly, it is reasonable to assume we are also capable of enormous production of fish. Having worked for CDFG, I can say with certainty that state workers often develop apathy and complacency in their fixed future of salary jobs. Private enterprise motivated by greater rewards for better production of salmon and steelhead would surely do a better job.

Commercial fishermen have historically harvested 84 percent of Klamath River salmon annually and by sheer logic of division of the resource should bear the brunt of the responsibility for rebuilding the fishery. Federal monies are available for grants to raise fish. When are we going to do it? When will we stop fighting amongst ourselves and spend that energy instead on what we all want – MORE FISH!

After Thought

Fishing is improving on the Klamath River and many groups can take part of the credit. We should all thank the United Anglers of California for doing the hard political work in Sacramento, the Pacific Coast Guides Association for its support of fisheries enhancement derbies for our sport fishing rights on the river. Organizations of anglers have increased the power and the voice of sport fishermen who comprise the largest number of users yet take the smallest percentage of fish harvested. I urge you to participate in the United Anglers of California 2830 Tenth Street, Suite No. 4 Berkeley, California 94710.

A mother osprey and her young sit on the nest. This is a common sight throughout the Klamath River Basin. Joe B. Clyburn photo

Bibliography

1. *Anadromous Fishes of California* By Donald H. Fry - 1973

2. *Lower Klamath Country* By Frances Turner McBeth - 1951

3. *Steelhead Fly Fishing and Flies* By Trey Combs 1976

4. Newspapers *Del Norte Record* - Del Norte County Museum *Del Norte Triplicate* - Triplicate Offices

5. Information on Safford's Island, Jim Gensaw and Captain Crone was provided by the Del Norte Historical Society

6. *The Family of Requa* By Amos Requa - 1898

The following tables are the compiled statistics of both the California Department of Fish and Game, and Gill Net Harvest Statistics by the U.S. Department of Fish and Wildlife.

Chinook Salmon Harvest

YEAR	INDIAN CHINOOK NET HARVEST	SPORT CATCH	OCEAN TROLL
1978	18,200	1,694	157,000
1979	13,650	2,141	196,650
1980	12,013	2,086	138,510
1981	33,033	3,983	128,280
1982	14,482	7,686	170,820
1983	7,890	4,342	54,150
1984	18,484	2,136	88,000

Estimated Total Angler Effort and Harvest, Lower Klamath River (Mouth To Johnson's [Km 30], Fall 1987)

Sample Location	Angler Trips	Angler Hours	Steelhead		Chinook		Coho	
			Half-pounders	Adults	Grilse	Adults	Grilse	Adults
MOUTH – HIGHWAY 101								
Mouth (Shore)	3,343	10,741	3	4	5	302	1	0
Boat Docks	22,949	68,793	95	39	141	2,153	0	0
SUBTOTAL	26,292	79,534	98	43	146	2,455	1	0
HIGHWAY 101 BRIDGE – BLAKES RIFFLE								
101 Bridge	9,673	36,296	524	408	679	1,686	23	42
Turwar Riffle	1,645	4,177	188	106	15	21	0	0
Turwar Ramp	8,745	39,968	956	965	1,542	2,787	51	91
Klamath Glen	3,720	13,899	389	150	602	885	2	12
Misc.	1,189	4,717	103	81	142	269	4	7
SUBTOTAL	24,972	99,047	2,160	1,710	2,980	5,648	80	152
TOTALS	51,264	178,581	2,258	1,753	3,126	8,103	81	152

Estimates of Hoopa Valley Reservation Indian gillnet harvest – 1987

CHINOOK SALMON (Numbers of fish)

Year	Area	Spring Race			Fall Race		
		Jack	Adult	Total	Jack	Adult	Total
1987	Estuary Commercial	0	0	0	0	29,040	29,040
	Estuary Subsistance	23	786	809	36	10,938	10,974
	Middle Klamath	5	171	176	30	5,079	5,109
	Upper Klamath	20	689	709	87	3,057	3,144
	Trinity River	122	4,146	4,274	262	4,982	5,244
1987	TOTAL	176	5,792	5,968	415	53,096	53,511

Klamath River adult inriver fall chinook run size, spawning escapement, sport catch, and Indian net harvest numbers and percent of the total inriver run size, 1978 to 1987.

	Spawning Escapement		Inriver Sport Catch		Indian Net Catch		Inriver Run
YEAR	NUMBERS	PERCENT	NUMBERS	PERCENT	NUMBERS	PERCENT	NUMBERS
1978	71,500	78	1,700	2	18,200	20	91,300
1979	34,300	68	2,100	4	13,700	27	50,100
1980	28,000	63	4,500	10	12,000	27	44,500
1981	38,300	49	6,000	8	33,000	43	77,300
1982	42,400	65	8,300	13	14,500	22	65,200
1983	45,700	79	4,300	7	7,900	14	57,900
1984	22,700	52	2,100	5	18,500	43	43,300
1985*	44,000	74	3,800	6	11,600	20	59,300
1986*	144,300	77	16,900	9	25,100	13	186,300
1987*	129,300	65	16,500	8	53,100	27	199,000

*Preliminary.

Klamath River Basin Fall Chinook Spawner Escapement, In-river Harvest and Run-size Estimates – 1986

SPAWNER ESCAPEMENT

Hatchery	Grilse	Adults	Totals
Iron Gate Hatchery	1,460	17,096	18,556
Trinity River Hatchery	3,699	15,268	18,967
SUBTOTALS	5,159	32,364	37,523

Natural	Grilse	Adults	Totals
Trinity River Basin (Above Willow Creek; excluding TRH)	21,919	91,088	113,007
Salmon River Basin	949	2,716	3,665
Scott River Basin	4,865	3,176	8,041
Shasta River Basin	683	3,274	3,957
Bogus Creek Basin	1,184	6,124	7,308
Main Stem Klamath River (Excluding Iron Gate Hatchery)	196	603	799
Misc. Klamath Tributaries (Above Hoopa Reservation)	606	4,919	5,525
SUBTOTALS	30,402	111,900	142,302
TOTAL SPAWNER ESCAPEMENT	35,561	144,264	179,825

IN-RIVER HARVEST

Angler Harvest	Grilse	Adults	Totals
Klamath River below Highway 101 Bridge	673	2,456	3,129
Trinity River Basin above Willow Creek	2,569	10,007	12,576
Balance of Klamath System	2,863	4,408	7,271
SUBTOTALS	6,105	16871	22,976

Indian Net Harvest	Grilse	Adults	Totals
Klamath River below Highway 101 Bridge	191	15,286	15,477
Klamath River – 101 to Trinity Mouth	377	5,033	5,410
Trinity River (Hoopa Square)	286	4,808	5,094
SUBTOTALS	854	25,127	25,981
TOTAL IN-RIVER HARVEST	6,959	41,998	48,957
TOTAL IN-RIVER RUN	42,520	186,262	228,782

Index

E

G

H

I

J

K

L

M

N

O